Tell Me a Story, I'll Bake you a Cake

by Joy Smith

AuthorHouse™
1663 Liberty Drive
Bloomington, IN 47403
www.authorhouse.com
Phone: 1 (800) 839-8640

Front Cover Design by Kim Hajas

Published by AuthorHouse 11/03/2016

ISBN: 978-1-5246-2494-1 (hc)
ISBN: 978-1-5246-2492-7 (sc)
ISBN: 978-1-5246-2493-4 (e)

Library of Congress Control Number: 2016914833

Print information available on the last page.

This book is printed on acid-free paper.

authorHOUSE®

Dedication

I want to thank my friends, relatives, neighbors, and strangers for the recipes I have begged, borrowed, or stolen over the years. Without them, this book wouldn't exist.

I also want to thank my husband's sixth grade teacher, Miss Moir, for making Marvin the grammar guru that he is today. Without Marvin's expertise, this book would be full of dangling participles and double negatives.

I especially thank all of you who have purchased my book. Without you I would have a huge stack of them in my garage.

Foreword

I'm the storyteller. You're the cook, but don't worry. The recipes in this book are simple. Many have spanned generations and stood the test of time.

You'll be entertained by my nostalgic stories about blizzards, church picnics, Lassie, Halloween kisses, and a magnificent cattle drive.

I've reversed the order of the chapters in my cookbook because of a lesson I learned in college. Eating dessert first is more than just decadence.

"Don't live your life on the left hand side of the menu," professor Clifford Dowdey told our creative writing class at the University of Richmond, Virginia, in 1966. This quote had nothing to do with food, but everything to do with life.

As you probably know, the typical menu has smaller, less expensive items on the left side: appetizers, soups, and salads. Entrees and desserts are on the right side: big, expensive, and rich.

Professor Dowdey wanted us to go out into the world and live life to the fullest. He encouraged us to think big, act boldly, and live richly. Don't let your aspirations be limited to the left side of the menu; that was his message.

I discovered that this advice is easier said than lived. It's hard to live big, act boldly, and live richly when you're teaching school, having babies, running carpools, going on school field trips, and attending track meets, baseball games, and soccer matches.

When I came up for air sometime in my mid-fifties, I was able to see the whole picture of my life. It was time to start taking Clifford Dowdey's advice seriously, and I have.

You'll find many details about my life as you read my personal stories. You'll discover that I grew up in Roanoke, Virginia, and that my father was a Baptist minister. Fishing, climbing trees, and being a cheerleader were some of my favorite activities. Special vacations were spent at my Uncle Harry's beautiful farm in Maryland visiting with Mother's sisters—the infamous Lavisson sisters—and playing with cousins.

I married my high school sweetheart Marvin Smith in 1966, and we had two children. Marvin's career took us Sleepy Hollow, New York, where we lived from 1979 to 1998. We now live in Fort Mill, South Carolina, and enjoy being back in the South even though the dreaded grits are served wherever we go.

In honor of Professor Dowdey, I'm going to begin this book with desserts and put appetizers last. I think he would like it that way. You will too, starting with the rich part.

DESSERTS

Whitney Smith's First Taste of Red Velvet Cake

Peggy's Red Velvet Cake

My friend Peggy Swink gave me her recipe for Red Velvet Cake sometime in the early 1970s. I know it had to be before 1976, because I made it for my daughter Whitney's first birthday party in May of that year. I have a picture of our little birthday girl, right after she put her face down into the cake. It's quite a "Kodak moment."

Peggy died suddenly, and unexpectedly, in June of 2003. She was 56.

I met Peggy when we bred our Cairn Terriers in 1971. When her husband came to drop off their dog "Toto" at our house, he not only delivered the dog, but also a lunch that Peggy had packed for her. I knew then and there that we'd be friends forever. Anybody who would pack a lunch for a dog was my kind of person.

What followed were two litters of adorable puppies and a lifetime friendship. Our children grew up together. So did we. Even though we were "geographically challenged" for almost twenty years, with the Smiths in New York and the Swinks in North Carolina, we remained close. Our visits together in August and at Christmas were a special tradition.

Our son attended Duke University and couldn't make it home for Easter one year, so naturally the Swinks invited him to their home for the holiday. Peggy made an Easter basket for him, as well as her Red Velvet cake.

Now she's gone, but reminders of her appear all around us. I'm especially aware of her when I find her handwritten recipes in my recipe box. I like to think of them as a rich legacy that will continue to bind our families together in the future.

Peggy's first grandchild was born almost exactly a year after she died. I'm pretty sure he had a red velvet cake for his first birthday party.

In Peggy's memory I'd like to share this very special recipe with you. Bon appétit.

Peggy's Red Velvet Cake

1/2 cup Crisco
1 1/2 cups sugar
2 eggs
2 tablespoons cocoa
2 oz. red food coloring
1 teaspoon salt
1 teaspoon vanilla
1 cup buttermilk
2 1/2 cups flour
1 1/2 teaspoons baking soda
1 tablespoon vinegar

Cream Crisco, sugar, and eggs. Make a paste of the cocoa and food coloring. Add to creamed mixture. Mix salt and vanilla with buttermilk and add to mixture, alternating with flour. Mix baking soda and vinegar and barely mix it into the batter.

Bake in two greased and floured 9-inch layer pans for 30 minutes at 350 degrees. Cool on a rack before frosting.

Frosting

5 tablespoons flour
1 cup milk
1 cup butter (not margarine)
1 cup sugar
1 teaspoon vanilla

In a saucepan on medium heat, cook flour and milk to a stiff paste. Let mixture sit until it gets cold. Cream butter and sugar. Add vanilla. Add to flour and milk paste and beat until it looks like whipping cream. Add a drop of red food coloring.

Serves 8

My tree was a solitary place to daydream, read books, and to eat lemons sprinkled with salt

Mother's Lemon Pie

As a child, I loved to climb trees—all kinds of trees. I remember them all fondly, even our neighbor's maple tree. I fell out of it one afternoon and knocked out my two front teeth (baby teeth, fortunately). It was a memorable event but didn't dampen my enthusiasm for tree climbing one bit.

My favorite tree, by far, was the large mimosa in our backyard. It spread over an entire corner of the yard and was magnificent in the summertime covered with fragrant pink pompom-like blossoms.

This tree had a nice low center of gravity for easy access and a wonderful spread of branches about halfway up that made a perfect little seat. When the leaves were full, I was pretty well-hidden from the world up there. I loved it.

My tree was a solitary place to daydream, read books, and to indulge in my favorite snack, lemons sprinkled with salt. I usually had a pocketful of lemons and a salt shaker with me when I climbed up to my perch. It sounds weird but I loved that sour, salty treat.

With this in mind, it should come as no surprise that Mother's lemon pie was one of my favorite desserts. It wasn't salty, but it sure was good. The creamy lemon filling was wonderfully tart and topped with fluffy meringue that practically melted in my mouth. It's the perfect dessert for lemon lovers like me.

I was happy to descend from the sanctuary of my tree and arrive at the dinner table on time, hands washed, when I knew we were having lemon pie for dessert. I was even happy to eat all the vegetables on my plate in order to have a slice. That says it all.

I'm all grown up now, and although my childhood mimosa tree died a long time ago, my love for it never did. Coincidentally, the two homes in which we raised our children had mimosa trees in the yard.

When we moved to South Carolina in 1998, we built a new home. I added two mimosa trees to the landscaping plan. They're beautiful and are just waiting to be climbed. I'm looking at them now, and for some reason, have a craving for Mother's lemon pie.

Mother's Lemon Pie

5 tablespoons flour
1/8 teaspoon salt
1 cup sugar
Zest of 1 lemon
Juice of 1 lemon
1 1/3 cups cold water
3 egg yolks, beaten
1 baked pie shell

In a saucepan, mix flour and salt with sugar. Grate rind from 1 lemon and add to sugar mixture along with lemon juice. Slowly stir in water and egg yolks. Cook on low heat and stir until it is the consistency of thick custard. Put aside and make meringue topping. Pour custard into baked pie shell and spread meringue on top, all the way to the edges.

Bake at 350 degrees until meringue is light brown, about 10 to 15 minutes. Let cool before slicing.

Meringue

2 egg whites
4 tablespoons sugar

Beat 2 egg whites until stiff. Add 4 tablespoons of sugar gradually until sugar is dissolved. Spread lightly over the custard filling.

Serves 6-8

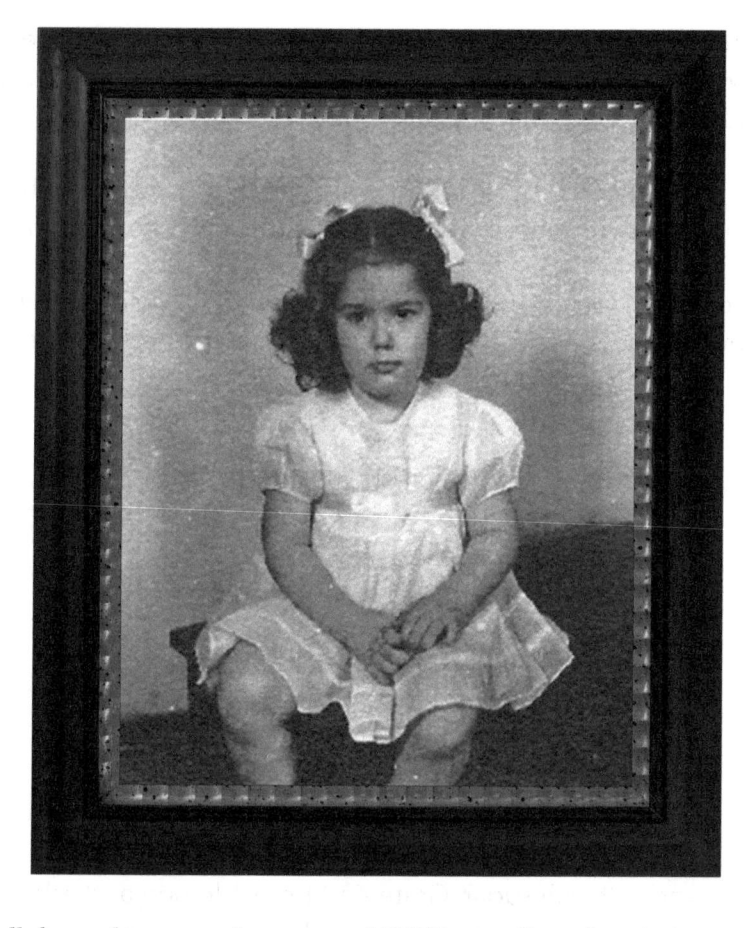

"I got all dressed to go on the train and NOW you tell me the trip is tomorrow?"

Apple Brown Betty

The Norfolk and Western Railroad was headquartered in Roanoke, Virginia, when I was growing up there. Trains were a way of life for all of us in Roanoke. We watched them by day as they crisscrossed the city, and lying in bed at night, we were lulled to sleep by the sound of train whistles in the distance—mournful, lonesome, and yet somehow comforting.

The N&W built sleek new steam engines at their shops in town. With names like The Powhatan Arrow and The Pocahontas, these magnificent locomotives were not only the workhorses that pulled loads of coal from the mountains to the coast, but also the gleaming engines that transported well-dressed passengers to destinations far and wide.

The train station downtown was an exciting place to be. As travelers hustled and bustled across the beautiful marble floors in the lobby, announcements of arrivals and departures reverberated throughout the building. All of this was exciting to a little girl in Sunday clothes anxious to see her aunts, uncles, and cousins at the other end of the line.

Equally exciting was the conductor standing outside the train consulting his pocket watch and shouting urgently, "All Aboard!" There was no doubt that he meant it too. Porters in white jackets helped us with our luggage.

I always sat next to the large window, nose pressed against it, watching with anticipation as we pulled away from the station. Our destination was always Washington, D.C., to visit my mother's family.

One of the best things about train travel was the dining car. The tables, covered with starched tablecloths, were set with china and silver. The waiters were courteous and attentive, and the menu featured entrees that made my mouth water. Watching the countryside pass by while eating a delicious meal was a unique experience I'll never forget.

Gone now from Roanoke are the steam engines, the N&W, and passenger service. Diesel engines replaced steam ones, the N&W moved to Norfolk and became the Norfolk Southern, and the train station closed.

Fortunately the station was restored and now houses a railroad museum. The museum features the incredible photographs of O. Winston Link, forever capturing the remarkable era of the legendary steam engine.

At the museum, I read about the dining cars and some of the great meals served on trains all over the country. I found a recipe that sounded familiar. It sounded like one that a little girl in Sunday clothes might have enjoyed in the dining car on her way to Washington, D.C.

I still love trains and always will. They're in my blood. There must be a rail line reasonably close to our house now because I occasionally hear a train whistle in the still of the night. It makes me smile.

Apple Brown Betty

10 – 12 apples, peeled, cored, and sliced
1 cup flour
2/3 cup sugar
1 cup brown sugar
1-2 tablespoons cinnamon
½ cup butter

Mix together flour, sugar, brown sugar, and cinnamon. Cut in cold butter until crumbs form. (I cheated and pulsed the mixture in my food processor a couple of times until it came together.)

Grease a 2-quart casserole dish with butter. Layer the apples in the dish until it's half full. Sprinkle half of the crumb mixture over the apples. Repeat with another layer of apples and remaining crumb mixture.

Bake at 375 degrees for 45 minutes or until the apples are tender. Serve warm with ice cream or whipped cream.

Serves 6

Peach fuzz = a spectacular Technicolor rash of Biblical proportions.

Peachy Keen Cobbler

I had a falling out with peaches when I was about ten years old and have never quite recovered from it.

I have to preface this story by mentioning that my skin is hypersensitive—bordering on weird, actually. All my life I've broken out in spectacular rashes, some of Biblical proportions, at the drop of a hat. Anything can set them off, it seems. Food, medicine, fabrics, grass, bugs, poison ivy, or even a change in laundry detergent can reduce me to an itchy, blotchy, Technicolor mess in minutes.

The peach incident was quite simple really. My father, a Baptist minister, took me peach picking one beautiful summer afternoon at the home of one of our church members. The members of our congregation were generous to our family with whatever they had to offer. In Mr. Grissow's case, it was peaches.

Clad in shorts, a halter top, and most assuredly barefoot, I happily scampered up and down Mr. Grissow's trees picking peaches in his small orchard. We ate cake, drank lemonade, had a nice visit, and left with baskets of fuzzy fruit in the trunk of the car.

On the way home my skin began to itch, and by the time we arrived home I was a pink nightmare. I was a victim of peach fuzz. Right then and there, I decided never to see, touch, or eat another peach as long as I lived.

That promise stayed intact until we moved to South Carolina in 1998, some 40 years later. Moving to the mecca of all things peaches can bring a shift in perception to even the most cynical critic. Rolling fields of pink-blossomed trees and baskets of luscious fruit for sale all around town can mellow a person.

I began to reacquaint myself with peaches, starting slowly with fresh peach ice cream and moving on to non-threatening jars of peach salsa. I finally took a leap of faith one evening at a local restaurant and ordered peach cobbler for dessert. To my relief, it was yummy, sweet, warm, and delicious—just like my mother used to make. I found her cobbler recipe and it's terrific. Keep in mind that this recipe works with any kind of fruit you like. It's sort of a "one recipe fits all" answer to dessert.

Serve it like Mother did—warm, with a scoop of ice cream on top, dusting it with a little sprinkle of nutmeg or cinnamon.

It's been a long journey for me, but thanks to this dish, I'm back in the fold of peach lovers. It's been worth the wait, that's for sure.

Peachy Keen Cobbler

6 cups peeled, diced peaches
1 cup sugar
½ cup all purpose flour
½ teaspoon baking powder
A pinch of salt
1 stick cold butter, cut into 8 pieces
1 egg
½ teaspoon vanilla extract

Toss the peaches with ½ cup of the sugar, and put into a greased baking dish (8-inch-square or 9- inch-round).

Put the flour, baking powder, salt, and ½ cup of sugar into a food processor and pulse once or twice. Add the butter and process for 10 seconds, until the mixture is well blended. By hand, beat in the egg and vanilla.

Drop this mixture, by the tablespoon, onto the fruit in the baking dish. Don't spread it out. Bake for 40 minutes in a 375 degree oven. Serve while hot. Top with vanilla ice cream or whipped cream if you like.

*Instead of peaches, you can substitute any fruit you like. Blackberries and blueberries are especially good in this recipe.

Serves 4-6

The Lavisson sisters with their mother
Left to right—Esther, Rena, Evelyn, Martha, Flora, and Mommie (seated)

Pots de Crème

I really don't have a sweet tooth and rarely think about dessert, except when company's coming. It's the salty, sour tastes that I crave. Chocolate, however, is the big exception. I just love it - the rich, dark, semi-sweet kind, that is.

Without exception my Aunt Flora's recipe for Pots de Crème is the best chocolate dessert I've ever eaten. It's simple and decadent. Most desserts that came from her kitchen were.

Aunt Flora was my favorite of Mother's four sisters. She, Uncle Harry, and my cousin Bonnie lived on what Daddy referred to as a "gentleman's farm" in Maryland. Their stately home was at the end of a long driveway, flanked by white fences and green pastures. Adjacent to the house was a big white horse barn.

I was lucky to spend my vacations at the farm when I was growing up. Aunt Flora was beautiful, gracious, and sophisticated. I wanted to be just like her. I learned the following lessons from my favorite aunt.

(1) If two little girls (Bonnie and I) want to dress cats in doll clothes and then take those cats for a ride in the car, you patiently drive them around, hoping the backseat upholstery doesn't get torn to shreds.

(2) You try to be a good hostess in spite of the fact that the pressure cooker has blown up and the kitchen ceiling is spattered with spaghetti sauce.

(3) When all those around you start dying their hair, it's okay to let yours go gray. Silver hair can be stunning and is a neutral color that goes with anything.

(4) The importance of appreciating family closeness, entertaining with ease, having fun, being stylish, honoring the wisdom that comes with age, and facing health issues with courage and devotion—all are lessons learned from Aunt Flora.

I think of her often. I have a large watercolor of the farm in our front hallway, pictures of her in family photo albums, a set of her dishes in the kitchen, and some of her recipes in my recipe box. Those recipes are very dear to me. Some are in her handwriting. All of them are fantastic. Her recipe for Pots de Crème is the one I use most.

This dessert is VERY rich, and a little goes a long way. It's perfect for a special occasion.

Pots de Crème is rich and elegant. Just like my Aunt Flora.

Pots de Crème*

3/4 cup milk
1 cup semi-sweet chocolate morsels
1 egg
2 tablespoons sugar
1 teaspoon vanilla
Pinch of salt
Whipped cream (I use the canned kind)

Heat milk to boiling point and add to blender containing all other ingredients. Blend on low for 1 minute. Pour into six demitasse cups or cordial glasses. About 1/3 cup per serving is just about right.

Chill overnight. Top with a dab of whipped cream and serve.

*At the bottom of my well-worn recipe card for Pots de Crème is a whimsical note from Aunt Flora. It says, "Serve with a candied violet, as the French often do." I had no idea what a candied violet was but found out it really is a candy violet. They come packed in small tins and are expensive and hard to find. Add this garnish if you like.

Serves 6

June Holcomb – 1972
She lived to be 100 years old and was still making her signature treat, Jets, in her nineties.

June's Jets

If you like rich dark chocolate rolled around a delicious butter cream filling, you're going to love June Holcomb's recipe for "Jets". I have no idea where this little treat got its name, but the end result is so good it doesn't matter.

June Holcomb was the mother of my childhood friend Tommy Holcomb. She reminded me of June Cleaver of "Leave it to Beaver" fame. Tommy's mother was always a sweet, well-dressed, stay-at-home mom, who worked hard keeping their Cape Cod style house as neat as a pin. She was also a great cook. Everybody loved her.

Tommy and I became friends as seventh graders at Woodrow Wilson Junior High School in Roanoke. As eighth graders, we starred in a class play in which our two characters kissed. It was my first kiss. We practiced a lot backstage to make the scene perfect. Right then and there, a lifetime friendship was born.

Years passed and we grew up, went to college, and married other people. The one thing that remained constant was Tommy's mother. She was still that sweet, well-dressed mom whom everybody loved. She hadn't missed a beat with her cooking skills, either.

The Holcombs had a Christmas Eve party at their home every year. It was a warm, intimate gathering of friends and family. My husband Marvin and I were fortunate to attend several times when we were in town. Mrs. Holcomb put out a dazzling array of food, including her signature butter cream treat, Jets.

I asked her for the recipe and was thrilled when she sent it to me. June Holcomb lived to be 100 years old. She was still making Jets in her nineties.

Now I'm the one who makes Jets for our Christmas party. My guests can devour a plate of Jets in a matter of minutes. So can yours.

If you want to make something that people lust after, make Jets. You'll be very popular.

June's Jets

1 16 ounce box confectioners powdered sugar
1/4 lb. butter
1/4 teaspoon salt
3 tablespoons evaporated milk
1 teaspoon vanilla
2 1/2 ounces unsweetened chocolate
1 tablespoon paraffin wax

Sift sugar. Combine with butter and salt. Add milk and vanilla and mix well. Roll in small balls and cool in refrigerator. Over very low heat, melt the chocolate and the paraffin together. With a toothpick, dip each ball into the chocolate mixture and place on waxed paper. Refrigerate until ready to serve.

Leaving For Vacation – 1949
"Are we there yet? Are we there yet?"

Peppermint Ice Cream

As I grew up, my family loaded up the car for vacation on August 1st and headed for Ednor, Maryland, to visit my Uncle Harry, Aunt Flora, and cousin Bonnie. Their beautiful home was on seventy acres of rolling hills called Mount Pleasant Farm. The farm was complete with horses, Black Angus cows, a barn, riding trails, a creek, air conditioning, and color TV.

I couldn't wait to get there. That was the problem. My father was notorious for his slow driving. Friends even joked with him about it, and his answer was always the same, "Better safe than sorry!"

Because Daddy did all the driving, the trips to the farm were agonizingly slow. Our car wasn't air conditioned, so imagine how uncomfortable it was on those sultry, August days. I was hot, miserable, and bored and became that annoying kid in the back seat asking over and over again, "Are we there yet? Are we there yet?"

Aside from the anticipation of getting to the farm at the end of the day, the only thing that helped me cope was knowing that we'd be stopping at a Howard Johnson restaurant for lunch. I watched anxiously to get a glimpse of their trademark orange roof.

The food didn't excite me. It was the ice cream. Howard Johnson was famous for their homemade ice cream—all twenty-eight flavors. My favorite was peppermint. It was luscious and creamy, with crunchy bits of peppermint candy mixed in it. Ice cream just didn't get any better than that.

Howard Johnson restaurants gradually disappeared over the years, as did peppermint ice cream. Some brands make a seasonal version of it at Christmas, but I think it's only mediocre.

I had given up hope of ever tasting the real thing again. Then to my surprise, an old cookbook had a recipe for peppermint ice cream. I decided to try it, with very low expectations for success.

First, the recipe sounded too easy. It didn't even require an ice cream machine. Just put the mixture in the freezer until it's solid, stirring periodically. It turned out great. The result was a fabulous frozen peppermint concoction that made me just as happy as Howard Johnson's ice cream did.

It's not exactly the same—nothing ever could be—but it's close enough to satisfy my craving for real peppermint ice cream. I think my question is finally answered. Yes, we're there now.

Peppermint Ice Cream

2 cups milk
1 pound hard peppermint candy
1 pint whipping cream

In a saucepan, combine milk and candy. Stir over medium heat until candy is dissolved. Chill.

Whip cream until firm and fold into chilled candy mixture in a metal bowl. Freeze for one hour. The mixture will separate, so stir it well to blend. I use a whisk. Return to freezer for another hour. Stir again until ice cream is smooth. Freeze for several hours or overnight.

Serve garnished with crushed peppermint candy.

Serves 6

Jackie and Joy
It's a chocolate lover's dream come true – especially without a mouthful of Novocain.

Jackie's Hot Fudge Sauce

Those of us who were in the high school class of 1962 were lucky to grow up when we did. It was a fascinating time of change in our society, and my classmates and I witnessed the beginnings of all sorts of things.

We experienced the infancy of television, the dawn of rock and roll music, the first man in space, and the "Cold War" with Russia. We wore bobby socks rolled down, collars turned up, danced the jitterbug, put peroxide on our hair, and watched newsreels at the movies.

We also had one unfortunate thing in common during these years. There was no fluoride in the water or sealants for our teeth back then, so we spent a lot of time at the dentist, getting cavities filled. Most of us have a mouth full of fillings.

On my semi-annual visit to Dr. Mattox, I could usually count on having a cavity filled. His office was in a medical arts building that had a luncheonette (a small restaurant) on the first floor.

After my appointment, my mother would always take me there for ice cream. I guess she felt sorry for me. We would sit at the soda fountain, and I would order a hot fudge sundae. Even though I was numb with Novocain, I loved those sundaes—especially the gooey, rich, hot fudge sauce. It almost made those visits seem worthwhile. Well, not really.

Even though I love hot fudge sundaes, I've never even considered learning how to make hot fudge from scratch. Pouring heated canned chocolate sauce over vanilla ice cream has worked just fine for me all these years. That is until we visited our friends, the Dolens, in Kingsport, Tennessee.

Jackie Dolen is a professional cook who had a catering business. She certainly knows her way around the kitchen, that's for sure. It's a treat visiting with the Dolens, and enjoying Jackie's home-cooked meals. I've asked for, and gotten, many of her recipes over the years.

My favorite is her hot fudge sauce. My husband asked me to get this recipe after she served it to us over pound cake for dessert. He had NEVER asked for a recipe before, so you know it must be good.

I think you'll agree that this is fabulous, any way you serve it. It's that wonderful, yummy, hot fudge sauce I remember, following my teenage dental visits. This decadent syrup is sure a lot more enjoyable without a mouth full of Novocain.

Serve this to someone you love for a special occasion, or give it as a gift. It's a chocolate lover's dream come true.

Jackie's Hot Fudge Sauce

6 ounce bag semi-sweet chocolate chips
1/2 cup butter
2 1/2 cups confectioners sugar
12 ounce can evaporated milk
1 teaspoon vanilla

Melt chocolate chips and butter over low heat. Add sugar and milk, blending well. Bring to a boil and cook for 8 minutes, stirring constantly. Add vanilla. Serve warm.

Makes 3 cups

How does this impossible dessert work? Nobody cares, as long as they get one.

Individual Baked Alaska

Baked Alaska is an oxymoron. The very name is a contradiction. It's one of those mysteries in life that delights us, however. We don't care that it doesn't make sense. All we care about is that it works, and we love the results.

The first time I ever saw this flamboyant dessert was as a kid on Christmas Eve. I remember it as if it were yesterday. Our house was beautifully decorated. The Christmas tree, covered with colored lights and hung with our favorite ornaments, had neatly wrapped gifts piled under it. White candle lights lit up the windows and mistletoe hung over the front door. The table displayed fresh greenery and red candles. We feasted on a wonderful Christmas Eve dinner together around that table.

When we were finished and the dishes had been cleared, Mother disappeared into the kitchen. We didn't know what dessert would be served, but we patiently waited, suspecting it was something special. We were right.

Mother came into the dining room with a Baked Alaska on a silver tray. We had no idea what it could be until she cut into it. I couldn't believe my eyes. The fact that ice cream was baked into a meringue shell seemed impossible, yet there it was. It had to be magic. It was definitely one of my mother's finest hours.

Ever since that night, Baked Alaska has claimed a special place in my heart. Because it's not one of those mainstream desserts that you see on a menu, I haven't eaten it in a long time. I never made one because I thought it would be too complicated.

So, imagine my excitement when I saw an easy recipe for individual Baked Alaskas. It never occurred to me that you could make several little ones instead of one big one. I immediately tried it and it worked. A new dessert was born in our house.

My mother's magnificent Baked Alaska has evolved into a dessert that I can actually make. You can too. How it works remains a mystery, but still nobody cares. All we care about is that it works, and we love the results. Some things never change.

Individual Baked Alaska

4 large sugar cookies (about 4 inches in diameter)*
4 scoops vanilla ice cream**
1/2 cup packed brown sugar
1/2 teaspoon cinnamon
4 egg whites
1/4 teaspoon cream of tarter

Place cookies on a baking sheet. Put a scoop of ice cream in the middle of each cookie. Freeze. Combine sugar and cinnamon. Beat egg whites and cream of tarter until soft peaks form (tips curl). Gradually beat in sugar mixture until stiff peaks form (tips stand straight). Spread over frozen ice cream and cookies, covering well. Put in freezer on baking sheet until ready to cook. Freeze up to 6 hours. Bake in a 500 degree oven for 3 minutes. Serve immediately.

Serves 4

* The cookies should be soft, not hard and crunchy. Use any kind of cookie you like, as long as they are the right size.

** Substitute ice cream flavors. Imagine a chocolate cookie with coffee ice cream or a peanut butter cookie with scoop of chocolate ice cream. Be creative!

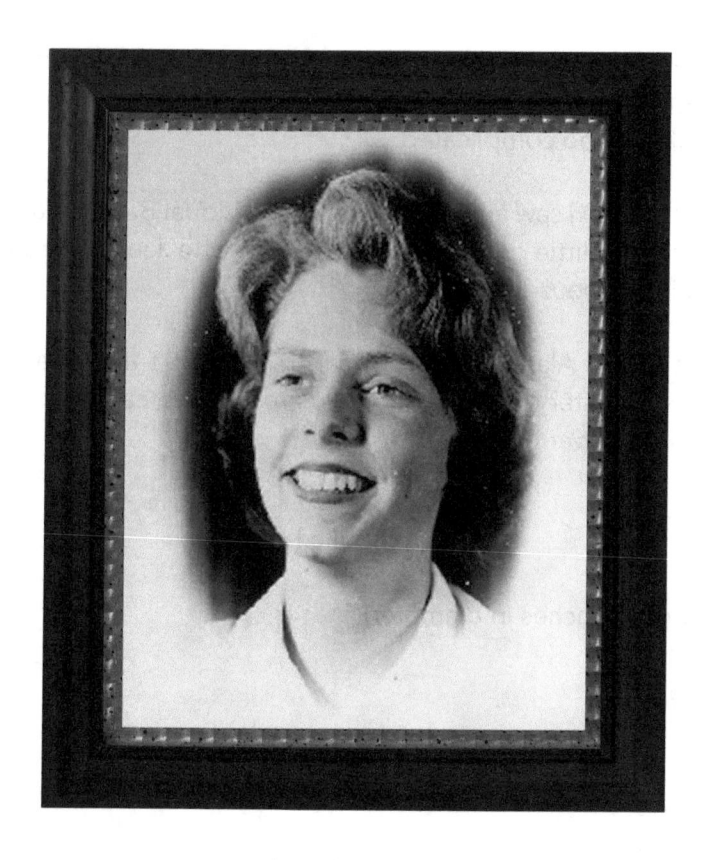

Loulie Johnston – 1961
We were tomboys as kids, silly as teenagers, and tried to be sophisticated as college girls.

Sugar and Spice Cookies

One of my best childhood friends was Loulie Johnston. We met in kindergarten and spent lots of time playing at each other's houses when we were kids.

We took Loulie with us on a few of our family vacations, and I got to spend time with her family at their cabin in the country. Their cabin, called "Lovit", was on a nice, deep, and rather secluded creek in the mountains of Virginia. It was there that I experienced the joys of skinny dipping and frog-gigging (not at the same time, however!). Another new adventure I had at "Lovit" was eating sweetbreads (pancreas) that Loulie's mother made for dinner. I had no idea what this was, but I loved it.

Loulie's favorite food at my house was my mother's sugar and spice cookies. Mother made a batch of them if she knew Loulie was coming over. Years later, mother even sent a "care package" of these cookies to Loulie when she was in college.

Loulie and I had a lot in common growing up. We were tomboys as kids, silly as teenagers, and tried to be sophisticated as college girls. We rode bikes and went fishing together, learned how to dance, flirt with boys, and were in the same high school sorority, the Sub Debs.

We grew up, got married, moved away, and had children who were about the same ages. When we returned home to visit our parents at the same time, our children had the opportunity to play together and become friends. Mother made her sugar and spice cookies for Loulie's children. The torch was passed to a new generation.

Loulie and I continued to visit each other's parents until they died. My parents passed away first. Loulie's father outlived her mother, and his death marked the end of an era. When we gathered at the Johnston's house after his funeral, I brought a plate of sugar and spice cookies for the family. I think my mother would have liked that.

I hope you'll make these cookies for someone you love and start your own tradition. Just be sure to save some for Loulie.

Sugar and Spice Cookies

1 1/2 cups Crisco
2 cups sugar
2 well-beaten eggs
1/2 cup molasses
4 cups flour
4 teaspoons baking soda
1/2 teaspoon salt
2 teaspoons cinnamon
1 1/2 teaspoons ground cloves
1 1/2 teaspoons ground ginger
Powdered sugar

Mix Crisco with sugar. Add eggs and molasses. Sift together flour, baking soda, salt, cinnamon, cloves, and ginger. Combine with creamed mixture. Chill dough.

Roll dough into balls about the size of a walnut. Drop dough by teaspoon onto a greased baking sheet about 2 inches apart. Bake at 375 degrees for 8-9 minutes. Remove from cookie sheet. Sprinkle with powdered sugar while warm.

Makes 6 dozen cookies

We spread icing and piped designs on the cookies, eating the broken ones as we worked.

Aunt Flora's Christmas Cookies

I'll never forget the Christmas my mother and I got snowed in at my Aunt Flora and Uncle Harry's farm in Maryland. I was about ten years old.

Mother and I traveled by train from our home in Roanoke, several days before Christmas. We went to enjoy the holiday with my aunt and uncle, my cousin Bonnie, and my grandmother.

My father was going to drive up on Christmas Eve, bringing all of our presents with him. It seemed like a good idea at the time.

The day after we arrived, we spent the afternoon making Aunt Flora's Christmas cookies. Mother and Aunt Flora did the baking, and Bonnie and I decorated them. The two of us spent hours spreading icing and piping designs on those cookies, eating the broken ones as we worked. We were up to our elbows in icing, colored sugar, and small decorative candies. We were in cookie heaven.

That night it began to snow. What could be more perfect? We were going to have a white Christmas. I felt like the luckiest little girl in the world.

We woke on Christmas Eve to howling wind and unbelievably heavy snow. It was a blizzard. We were snowed in. Daddy was snowed out. The enormity of this fact didn't sink in until Christmas morning.

Except for the gift from my aunt and uncle, I had no presents to open. The sad truth was that I was a kid without presents in the midst of lavish gift giving. The climax of the morning came when Aunt Flora got a mink stole.

After they opened their presents, things began to look up. Following a hearty breakfast, Bonnie and I spent the day tunneling through snowdrifts so deep we could stand in them. We made snow ice cream, drank hot chocolate, played games, sang along to Christmas records on the stereo, and ate LOTS of those wonderful cookies.

Late that afternoon, the family gathered in the dining room for a beautiful candlelit dinner, which featured prime rib roast and Baked Alaska for dessert.

Daddy got through to us the next day, and we celebrated Christmas again. This time it was my turn. When Mother, Daddy and I left to go home, Aunt Flora gave me some of her cookies for the road.

I make those cookies now, and whenever I do, I'm reminded of that Christmas. Even without gifts, Christmas came that day. Strangely, I think it might have been one of the best ever.

In the spirit of Christmas, and in Aunt Flora's memory, I want to give the gift of her cookies. The only thing missing from the recipe is a blizzard.

Aunt Flora's Christmas Cookies

1/2 cup butter
1 cup sugar
1 egg, well beaten
1 1/2 cups flour
2 teaspoons baking powder

Cream butter and sugar together. Add egg. Sift together flour and baking powder and gradually add to other ingredients. Roll into a ball. Chill.

On a floured surface, roll dough 1/8-inch thick (or less) and cut with cookie cutter. With a metal spatula transfer to a greased cookie sheet. Bake 8 minutes at 325 degrees. Cool slightly before removing from pan.

Decorator's Icing

4 tablespoons shortening
3 cups powdered sugar
2 egg whites
1/2 teaspoon vanilla

Cream shortening and half of the sugar. Beat for 2 minutes. Beat egg whites until the tips curl and hold their shape and add to mixture, along with the vanilla and the rest of the sugar. Cream well. If too stiff, add a little water. If too thin, add more powdered sugar.

Makes 2 ½ dozen cookies

Mother and Daddy's 25th Anniversary—October, 1955
Her popcorn balls are cleverly hidden behind the cake.

Mother's Popcorn Balls

Halloween was, without a doubt, the most exciting night of the year for me and my friends when I was a kid. What could be better than roaming through the neighborhood in disguise begging for candy? Three magic words, "Trick or Treat", opened the floodgates of all kinds of wonderful sweet surprises—and the occasional apple, which we immediately threw away.

Halloween was the ultimate combination of mischief, greed, and unbridled joy. At the end of the night, much like a pirate counting his gold, we appraised our loot at the kitchen table, sampling most of it. The resulting sugar rush was exhilarating.

My mother always made popcorn balls to give out on Halloween. It became her trademark. She loved to tell about the little boy who knocked on the front door several days before Halloween to ask if she was going to make her popcorn balls again. He wanted to get there early to get one. She said yes and never failed to keep her promise every year after that.

One of my favorite Halloween memories is of our neighbor, Mildred Irvin. She was a good friend of our family and a member of our church where my father was the minister. Mildred absolutely loved Halloween and was known to dress up and go "trick-or-treating" herself. A petite woman, she just bent down and blended in with a group of children without being detected. She had a great sense of humor and loved to play a good trick on someone. That someone was my father and Halloween was her golden opportunity. Every year she managed to sneak into our house with a bunch of kids, yell "Surprise!", and give my father a big kiss on the cheek. It was a tradition we all laughed about, and she got to tell everybody at church about kissing the preacher.

I get nostalgic about Halloween, remembering the thrill of the hunt on those chilly autumn nights as if it were yesterday. It's in that spirit of Halloween that I've carried on mother's tradition of giving out popcorn balls. I like to think that Mildred Irvin's spirit still lives on Halloween night playing tricks on people. I like to think of Daddy sitting in his living room chair waiting for his surprise Halloween kiss.

Years ago a little boy in our neighborhood stopped by our house before Halloween to ask if I was going to make popcorn balls again. He said he and his friends wanted to know so they could get some. I think my mother sent him.

Mother's Popcorn Balls

10 cups popcorn
1 cup sugar
1/2 cup water
1/4 cup molasses
1 teaspoon vinegar
1/2 teaspoon salt
1 tablespoon butter

Put sugar, water, molasses, vinegar, and salt in a saucepan and stir to mix. Using a candy thermometer heat mixture to 265 degrees. Stir in butter. Remove from heat and pour over popcorn. Butter your fingers and form into balls.

Makes approximately 10 balls

Old Fashioned Popcorn Balls*

5 quarts popped corn
2 cups sugar
1 1/2 cups water
1/2 teaspoon salt
1/2 cup light corn syrup
1 teaspoon vinegar
1 teaspoon vanilla

Butter sides of a medium size saucepan. Add sugar, water, salt, corn syrup, and vinegar and stir. Using a candy thermometer cook to hardball stage (250 degrees). Stir in vanilla. Slowly pour over popcorn, stirring slightly to coat popcorn. With buttered hands, shape into balls. Cool on rack and lightly salt them.

*I sometimes use this recipe as an alternative to Mother's. Both are good, but this one makes more.

Makes 15-20 balls

MEATS

Mount Pleasant Farm – Ednor, Maryland
Ground Zero for the infamous Lavisson sisters

Fool Proof Roast

My mother, born in 1905, was the middle child of five sisters—the infamous Lavisson sisters of Washington, DC. My cousin Neil described the sisters as "crusty old broads". He wasn't far off the mark either-except for Aunt Flora. While the other sisters could strike fear into us with "the look" or a well-chosen word, Aunt Flora was gentle and sweet—at least to me she was.

I loved my aunts (and mother too, of course), but I adored Aunt Flora. She was beautiful, sophisticated, witty, stylish, graceful—and rich.

Uncle Harry owned a lucrative contracting business in the District of Columbia. His home reflected his success. The house, with large white columns, was on a beautiful farm in the rolling hills of Maryland. I loved it there.

The farm was an amazing place to spend vacations several times a year. I played croquet on the manicured lawn with my cousins, went horseback riding, and hiked through the pastures and the woods. The big white barn had haylofts to climb, a big rope to swing on, a tack room that smelled of polished leather, and stalls downstairs for the horses.

I enjoyed all of these things, as well as being with my relatives. Yes, those relatives—the Lavisson sisters. With the exception of my mother, the sisters lived in the Washington, D.C, area. Consequently, the farm was ground zero for family reunions. This was a good thing.

There were picnics, square dances in the barn, and parties. Aunt Flora was the consummate hostess. Lots of good food came out of her kitchen during these events. Entertaining seemed effortless for her.

I grew up in awe of my favorite aunt. She became my role model in life. I've tried to be like her as best I can. I even let my hair go gray because Aunt Flora's silver hair was gorgeous. I figured if it was good enough for her, it was good enough for me. And so it is.

I don't have any sisters like Aunt Flora did or a farm with horses, but I do have some of her recipes and a nice kitchen to cook them in. My favorite recipe of hers is called Fool Proof Roast. It's an expensive dinner, so save this one for a special occasion. With only three ingredients, it might be the easiest recipe you've ever made. Expensive, yes. Difficult, no.

Aunt Flora served her roast for a family dinner party one evening at the farm. Even the Lavisson sisters were on their best behavior that night. I remember it well.

Fool Proof Roast*

Standing Rib Roast (any size)
Salt, Pepper
Garlic powder (optional)

Plan to cook the meat in the morning. Allow several hours to lapse between steps 1 and 2.

(1) Have the roast at room temperature. Preheat the oven to 375 degrees. Rub roast with seasonings and place on a rack, rib side down, in a roasting pan. Cook for I hour at 375 degrees. Turn the oven off. DO NOT OPEN OVEN DOOR!!!
(2) 30-40 minutes before serving time, turn the oven on again at 375 degrees and cook roast. Remove from oven and let rest for 5 minutes before carving so that the juices remain inside the roast. The meat will be medium rare. (If you want your meat to be well done, cook for an additional 15-20 minutes before serving.)

* Trust this recipe. It works. If you add more cooking time, you can overcook and ruin a perfectly nice rib roast.

The Lavisson Sisters
(Left to right – Esther, Rena, Martha, Flora, Evelyn)

Aunt Esther's Swedish Meatballs

Aunt Esther was the youngest of my mother's four sisters. She was beautiful with an infectious laugh and a wicked sense of humor. I just couldn't help but love her.

Aunt Esther lived in Wheaton, Maryland, with my Uncle Teddy and my cousins, Neil and Patricia. I had a great time visiting them. I remember playing with Neil and his friends, riding bikes in the neighborhood, and adopting a Cocker Spaniel puppy from their next-door neighbor. I named the puppy "Buff", and he was my constant companion when I was growing up. One memory of visiting Aunt Esther wasn't so fond, however.

It was the fall of 1954, and Hurricane Hazel swept through the area while we were there. Hazel's howling winds and torrential downpours were pretty scary to a fourth grader—maybe to the grown-ups too. I have vivid memories of that storm to this day.

What I don't remember about Aunt Esther was her cooking. I know that her kitchen was used, however, because there was a really weird dishwasher next to the sink. It loaded from the top and I don't think it worked. It was just there to drain the dishes washed by hand, and it was always full of dishes.

Even though I don't remember Aunt Esther busying around the kitchen whipping up dinner, I have written proof of her cooking skills. I have her recipe for Swedish meatballs, which is a favorite of ours.

There's nothing Swedish about Aunt Esther's meatballs, but they sure are good. Traditional Swedish meatballs are served in a sour cream sauce. Aunt Esther's are simmered in a combination of grape jelly, lemon juice, and chili sauce. It sounds odd, but it's really good.

I've been serving these meatballs at our annual Christmas party for years. I can't imagine the party without them, as a matter of fact. Apparently neither can our guests. It doesn't seem to make any difference how many I make, they're all gone at the end of the night, a tribute to their goodness.

These meatballs take a bit of preparation time, especially if you're making a lot of them. I usually double the recipe for a big party of 40 to 50 people. The good news is that you can make them days in advance of your big party, or a "do" as my husband calls it.

Swedish or not, serve up some of Aunt Esther's meatballs for your next "do". You'll be lucky if you have a couple of them left for yourself at the end of the night.

Aunt Esther's Swedish Meatballs

2 pounds lean ground beef
1 egg
1 onion, grated
Salt, pepper
Mix ingredients together well. Roll into bite size meatballs.

Sauce

12 ounce bottle chili sauce
Juice of 1 lemon
16 ounce jar grape jelly

In a large saucepan, stir ingredients together over medium low heat until jelly is melted. Add meatballs, and simmer until browned, about 15-20 minutes.

Serve immediately in a chafing dish, or cool and store in the refrigerator for several days. Just reheat and serve at your convenience.

Serves 20-25

Joy and Neil on horseback at Mount Pleasant Farm—1966
Sitting high in their saddles, they mounted a magnificent cattle drive.

Beef O'Keefe

My cousin Neil O'Keefe was a real character. You never knew what he might say, but you knew it would be funny. Even as a little kid, he had a mischievous quality about him. Thankfully, he never outgrew it.

Apparently Neil and I were very much alike, because our mothers used to say that it looked like we were "up to something". They were probably right.

I have so many happy memories of time spent with Neil. As kids we rode horses at our Uncle Harry's farm in Maryland. As teenagers we cruised around without a care in Neil's beloved Austin Healy. As grown-ups we continued to have fun together. Fortunately Neil's wife and my husband enjoyed it, too. As married couples, we created a lot of new stories to laugh about.

Neil and I had lots of adventures together, but one in particular landed us in hot water with Uncle Harry. His farm, aptly named Mount Pleasant, was actually a 70-acre estate with white fenced pastures, horses in the barn, and cows grazing in the fields.

Like most kids our age we were big cowboy fans. While riding horses one day we got the irresistible urge to mount a cattle drive. Sitting high in our saddles, we chased those cows (lots of them) from one end of the farm to the other and back again. It was a magnificent cattle drive by any standards.

Unfortunately these "cows" were Uncle Harry's Angus cattle, prized for their marbled beef. Apparently we were running the fat off of them. Uncle Harry was mad, we were grounded, and the cows once again grazed peacefully in their pastoral surroundings.

We grew up, but never grew apart. Neil went to Vietnam and regaled us with stories of his adventures there. He had unorthodox political views and unique opinions on controversial topics, all of which he shared with gusto. My cousin was not dull.

Neil had a myriad of interests, one of which was tinkering in the kitchen. He created a delicious dish he called "Beef O'Keefe". It was an uncommonly good combination of pasta, vegetables, ground beef, garlic, and barbeque sauce. I asked for the recipe but he said he didn't have one because he just threw things together until it tasted right.

Neil died of cancer in 2006. We talked often during his illness, laughing a lot about our escapades over the years. One day I asked him to recreate the recipe for Beef O'Keefe for me, which he did. I never thought to ask him, but I wonder if he used Angus beef in this recipe. Hmmm….

Beef O'Keefe

1 pound sirloin steak, cut into bite size pieces
2-3 cloves garlic, minced
3 tablespoons olive oil
½ cup chopped onion
½ cup sliced mushrooms
1 green pepper, cut into ¼ inch strips
One 10 ½ ounce can cream of tomato soup
¼ cup (or more) hot barbeque sauce

Brown meat and garlic in olive oil. Remove from pan. Add onion and mushrooms and sauté until softened. Add meat, peppers, tomato soup and barbeque sauce to taste. Stir and simmer for about 20 minutes. Serve over egg noodles.

Serves 4

Marvin's trip to the store for milk: He returned with a big hat and a tall beer.

Marvin's Favorite Meatloaf

My husband loves meatloaf. I mean, he really LOVES meatloaf. I think I could serve it to him every day with mashed potatoes and green beans, and he'd be in Heaven.

I even made him a heart-shaped meatloaf one year for Valentine's Day. I covered it with barbecue sauce and baked it. It was colorful, zesty, and perfect. He was thrilled.

I've been told that meatloaf became popular during the lean years of the Depression and during World War II, when meat was rationed. Housewives across America began adding fillers to make meat go further. The rest is history. Meatloaf found a permanent place in our culture.

There are more variations in meatloaf recipes than I can count. Lord knows, I've tried most of them. The traditional one that my Mother made contained ground beef, dried onion soup mix, cracker crumbs, minced onion, catsup, and an egg. I grew up eating it and loved it.

In recent years, this old-fashioned comfort food has been rediscovered and reinvented. With the addition of savory ingredients, such as wild mushrooms, roasted peppers, chilies and fresh herbs, and meats such as ostrich and buffalo, meatloaf has a new reputation for being positively upscale.

There are basically two ways to cook meatloaf. You can form it into a loaf (or a heart shape), and cook it in a baking dish, or you can put it into a loaf pan to bake. There are two schools of thought on this issue. One school maintains that cooking meatloaf in a freeform loaf shape can dry it out. The other thinks that cooking meatloaf in a loaf pan can leave fatty liquids in the pan, and make it greasy. I think it's good either way.

The recipe I'm sharing with you is Marvin's favorite meat loaf. It's different from any other I've tried. This one is baked in a loaf pan, with a rather unusual sauce poured over it. This is definitely not my mother's meatloaf.

This dish has become so popular with our friends that Marvin's name is synonymous with meatloaf. People actually stop him on the street to tell him how much they like his meatloaf. Marvin is famous for MY recipe.

If you want to make someone happy on Valentine's Day (or any day), make Marvin's favorite meatloaf. It worked for me.

Marvin's Favorite Meat Loaf

1 medium onion
3 slices bread
1 egg, beaten
1 1/2 teaspoons salt
1 1/4 teaspoons pepper
1 teaspoon Worcestershire sauce
1 teaspoon dry mustard
8 ounce can tomato sauce, divided
1 1/2 pounds lean ground beef
2 tablespoons vinegar
2 tablespoons water
1 tablespoon Dijon mustard
2 1/2 tablespoons brown sugar

Mince onion. Tear bread into crumbs with a fork. Add bread crumbs, onion, egg, salt, pepper, Worcestershire sauce, dry mustard, and 1/2 cup tomato sauce to ground beef. Mix together lightly but thoroughly. Pack mixture into a 9x5x3 inch loaf pan.

Mix the remaining tomato sauce with the vinegar, water, mustard, and brown sugar. Pour over the meat. Bake at 350 degrees for 1 1/2 hours, uncovered. Remove from oven and let sit for 5 minutes. Slice and serve.

Serves 6

Jenny, whose Cocker Spaniel loved Michael Jackson

Jenny's Pepper Steak

I met my sister-in-law, Jenny, in 1962. I was a senior in high school when she married my brother. Jenny and I became instant friends. She was only a year ahead of me in school, but light years ahead in maturity. After all, she was married, and I was just getting ready to go off to college.

Jenny was learning how to be a wife, how to keep a house, and how to cook. I, however, was learning how to live in a dorm with a bunch of girls, going to fraternity parties, and trying to pass math.

Years passed. She had children. I graduated from college and got married. We had very different lives, but it didn't matter. We were like sisters and shared lots of good times together.

Although Jenny and my brother ultimately divorced, it didn't matter. My friendship with Jenny continued, as did the good times.

During one of my visits with Jenny, her ill-behaved cocker spaniel got into my luggage and ate a Michael Jackson CD, a bottle of blood pressure pills, and a huge Swiss chocolate bar. Against all odds, the dog lived.

The night that Jenny and my husband were trying to light her new gas grill was also memorable. Jenny caught her hair on fire while leaning over to see if the grill was lit. It was. She wasn't hurt but looked strange for a while without her bangs.

Over the years, Jenny evolved into a good cook. Her specialty was Southern green beans, Marvin's favorite. When we were planning a visit she started cooking a pot of beans days in advance. She cooked them slowly with a ham hock, the old fashioned way. They were unbelievably good. We didn't call her the "Green Bean Queen" for nothing.

Jenny had a lot to do with teaching me how to cook. After all, she got a head start on me, so I learned from her. I've got a number of her recipes in my collection and think of her when I make them. She died in 2003, so her handwritten recipe cards are very special to me.

One of my favorites is her recipe for Pepper Steak. It was one of the first things I learned to cook, so you know it's easy. If you want a simple dish with lots of flavor, try this one. Hopefully, a cocker spaniel won't eat it before you do.

Jenny's Pepper Steak

4 cups cooked rice
1 1/2 pounds round steak, cut into bite sized pieces
1 teaspoon paprika
2 tablespoons butter
2 cloves garlic, minced
10 ½ ounce can beef broth
1 large onion, sliced
2 green peppers, sliced
1/4 cup water
1/4 cup soy sauce
2 tablespoons cornstarch

Sprinkle steak with paprika, and brown in butter. Add garlic, broth, and onion, and simmer for 1 1/2 hours. Add green peppers, and simmer for another 30 minutes. Blend water, soy sauce, and cornstarch, and stir into meat mixture until thickened. Serve over rice.

Serves 4

Nancy and Joy – 1966
Proud leaders of the annual P.E.A. (Party Every Afternoon) "Tapping In" Ceremony

Nancy's Flank Steak Marinade

I got one of the best recipes in my collection from my college roommate Nancy Saunders. Nancy and I roomed together for the four years we attended Westhampton College, the University of Richmond women's college. It didn't take us long to figure out that no one else could possibly stand to room with either one of us, so we stuck it out together the whole time.

We became very close friends. The old saying, "You'll always be my best friend because you know too much," is an understatement in our case. We were partners in crime from the very beginning.

When we were there, Westhampton had strict and totally outdated rules, most of which we decided didn't apply to us. These rules were discontinued a couple of years after we graduated in 1966, proving that timing in life is everything.

You won't believe this but -

(1) We had to sign in and out of the dorm when leaving campus.
(2) We could go out with guys only on specific "date nights" (Friday-Sunday and Wednesdays) and there was a midnight curfew—11:00 pm on Wednesday.
(3) If we spent a night away from campus, we could only stay in "approved homes," recommended by our parents.

(4) There was a demerit system—too many demerits and you were grounded.

(5) A woman named Miss Stewart inspected the dorm rooms for neatness, leaving on our door many a disparaging note, which we ignored.

(6) There was no drinking on campus. The unintended consequences of this rule meant that students drank in town, and then drove back for the fraternity parties on campus. Not a good idea.

Although there were fraternities at Richmond College, there were no sororities at Westhampton. This was easily solved by a group of girls, years ahead of us, who enjoyed a robust social life. They simply made up a sorority, and aptly named it "PEA" (Party Every Afternoon). The annual "tapping in" ceremony was a highly anticipated, and somewhat bawdy, event. Nancy and I were proud members.

After graduation, Nancy and I went our separate ways but were never out of touch with each other. We both got married and enjoyed spending time together as couples.

On one of our visits to see Nancy, she cooked an outstanding meal that we'll never forget. It was marinated flank steak on the grill, and it was extraordinary. We had never tasted a steak remotely as good as that one. Naturally I got Nancy's recipe and have been making it ever since, much to the delight of everyone who has tasted it.

This marinade is not only great with flank steak, but also London broil and shish kabob. If you want the ultimate marinade, try this one. Nancy's recipe remains as good as gold, just as our friendship. Both are classics.

Nancy's Flank Steak Marinade

½ cup oil
¼ cup soy sauce
1 tablespoon brown sugar
1 minced garlic clove (or more if you like)

Mix ingredients together and pour over the steak. Puncture the meat all over with a sharp fork so the marinade can penetrate. Put it in the refrigerator for several hours, turning periodically. I usually marinate it in the morning and leave it in the refrigerator all day. The longer it sits, the better it gets.

Baste the steak with the marinade while it's cooking. Remember, marinated meat cooks faster than a regular steak, so be careful not to overcook it.

Let the steak sit for a few minutes before cutting it on the diagonal to serve. Enjoy the best flank steak you've ever eaten.

Makes ¾ cup of marinade

Chris and Joy—friends on the tennis court and off. WAY off the court!

Chris's Mother's Peppered Ribeye Roast

I started playing tennis in the seventh grade on the asphalt courts behind my junior high school. I played with my friends, using my father's wooden racket. It was rudimentary tennis, but tennis nevertheless.

Sadly, my tennis hasn't improved much since those days, but my enthusiasm for the game has. I still love it.

Other sports are just not for me. I tried running and biking in the 1970s, but the combination of heat, rain, and dogs chasing me ended those endeavors. Swimming laps was boring and the treadmill was monotonous. However, if you put a racket in my hand and ask me to chase a little yellow ball around a tennis court, I can do that all day long.

Tennis has been a great way to meet people over the years wherever we've lived. I've made a number of good friends through tennis. After all, we share a love for the game and enjoy time spent on the court together, whether it's competitive team play or just for fun.

When women play socially, more than tennis takes place on the court. Players learn more about each other than just their tennis skills. Stories are shared, jokes are told, and recipes are exchanged. I think these games are actually group therapy with a few hours of tennis thrown in for good measure.

I met one of my best friends, Chris Rigney, on the tennis court. We took lessons together sometime in the 1980s and have been friends ever since. Our friendship even took us to the bottom of the world on a National Geographic Expedition to Antarctica in 2014, minus our tennis rackets, of course.

Chris is a natural athlete. It didn't take long to figure out that she was a lot better tennis player than I was.

She might be the better player, but I'm a better cook. We all have our strong points—mine just happen to be in the kitchen. One of my favorite recipes comes from Chris's kitchen, however. It's her mother's recipe for peppered ribeye roast, and it's great.

This dish is perfect for company. The roast has a peppery crust on the outside, and the gravy that accompanies it is a flavorful combination of pan drippings and marinade.

Any way you serve it, this recipe is an ace.

Chris's Mother's Peppered Ribeye Roast*

5-6 pound boneless ribeye roast, fat trimmed off
1/4 cup coarsely cracked pepper
1/2 teaspoon ground cardamom
1 tablespoon tomato paste
1/2 teaspoon garlic powder
1 teaspoon paprika
1 cup soy sauce
3/4 cup vinegar

Combine pepper and cardamom and press into all sides of the roast. Place in a baking dish. Make a sauce from the last 5 ingredients and pour into the baking dish with the meat. Marinate in the refrigerator for 24 hours, spooning sauce over the meat several times.

Remove roast from refrigerator, and let sit for 1 hour until it's room temperature. Strain and reserve marinade. Wrap roast in foil and bake in shallow pan for 2 hours at 300 degrees. The meat will be medium rare. Open foil, and reserve pan drippings. Put the roast back into the oven, uncovered, and turn the temperature up to 350 degrees. Let it brown while you're making the gravy.

Gravy

For the gravy, combine 1 cup pan drippings with 1/2 cup marinade and 1/2 cup water and bring to a boil. Mix 1 tablespoon cornstarch into 1/4 cup cool water. Gradually stir into gravy to thicken it.

Remove roast from oven. Let sit for 5 minutes before slicing. Serve with gravy.

*The leftovers are delicious served on rolls with horseradish sauce.

Lois celebrates first place with her favorite motorcycle gang
Beer, brisket, cool dudes, and a blue ribbon - what could be finer?

Blue Ribbon Barbecued Beef Brisket

I have one of the best recipes in my collection all because our friend Lois Way spent 1988 in Texas. After only 12 months in the Lone Star State, she returned home to Virginia, but thankfully she didn't return empty-handed.

She brought back something priceless, something that people lust after and hunger for, something indigenous to Texas—the recipe for barbecued beef brisket. Once I tasted it, there was no going back to any other recipe for it. This was "hands down" the best barbecued beef I'd ever tasted.

Fortunately for all of us, during her short stay in Texas, Lois attended a good old-fashioned barbecue where this mouth-watering Southwestern specialty was served. She asked the hostess for the recipe, and was surprised to find that it wasn't cooked on the grill like all the other foods had been, but it had been slow baked in the oven.

The brisket is marinated overnight in some really interesting ingredients and then baked slowly for 6 to 7 hours in the oven. Believe me, well before it's done, your house will smell so good you can hardly stand it. I've had friends stop by my house when this is in the oven and they just HAVE to know what's cooking. Some have even come back later for a taste. All have asked for the recipe.

A large barbecued brisket will feed a hungry crowd and leave them begging for more. One friend of mine baked it ahead of time and took it to a family reunion. Another took it to feed a large group of friends at the beach. I featured it at a July 4th party at our home and the results were all the same—overwhelming success.

Lois scored the ultimate win with this recipe. Her office had a barbecue cook-off contest and apparently there was a lot of preliminary bragging going on about who would win. One fellow even hauled in a really big grill from Texas for the event.

Lois, of course, won. It just goes to show that big fancy equipment isn't everything. The best recipe will always win.

Take my word for this—unless you're a vegetarian, you're going to love this barbecue favorite. Kudos to Lois and the great state of Texas. Yee-haw!

Blue Ribbon Barbecued Beef Brisket

5 pound beef brisket
1 tablespoon liquid smoke
2 tablespoons Worcestershire sauce
1 tablespoon garlic salt
1 tablespoon onion salt
1 teaspoon black pepper
1 cup of your favorite barbecue sauce

Mix liquid smoke and Worcestershire sauce. Brush brisket with mixture. Combine dry spices and sprinkle over brisket. Cover and refrigerate overnight.

Roast at 250 degrees for 6-7 hours, covered. Spread barbecue sauce over brisket for the last hour. Uncover for the last 1/2 hour.

Let cool. Cut meat on the diagonal. Serve on small party rolls as an appetizer or large rolls as a main dish. Drizzle some sauce from the pan over the sandwiches for additional flavor.

They were last seen driving on the Autobahn at 150mph—1972

The German Dish

In 1972, my husband and I took a three-week trip to Germany, Switzerland, and Austria. We were young, footloose, and fancy-free and traveled on our own by car and train. We stayed in small hotels and some private homes along the way and believe it or not, used a book called "Europe on $5 and $10 a Day" as our guide.

We were awed by the cathedrals in Cologne and Vienna and the magnificent castles we saw while traveling down the Rhine River. We drove through the Black Forest, toured a salt mine deep inside a mountain in Salzburg, and stayed on beautiful Lake Constance in Germany and Lake Lucerne in Switzerland. We went to the top of majestic Mount Pilatus by tram and rode the Orient Express from Vienna to Munich, where we attended Oktoberfest. It was a fantastic experience.

A poignant moment in our trip came when we visited the Olympic Village in Munich. There was a makeshift memorial—a fence covered with flowers—for the Israeli athletes who were murdered by Palestinian terrorists just weeks before our arrival.

I kept a journal each day, including the meals we ate. We ate well, that's for sure. From my notes, I know we tried (and loved) the local food, wine, and beer from each region we visited. We used a German/ English dictionary to translate the menus, which worked pretty well, but it wasn't foolproof. At one restaurant an entree translated into "a meal of arthritis"! We chose not to order it.

Of the meals we did order, my favorite was herring in sour cream, and Marvin's was bratwurst. He loved all the different sausages and ate his way across Germany, trying them all.

When we got home, I wanted to replicate some of the delicious meals we enjoyed on our trip. I found a recipe called "Kielbasa and Potatoes" that sounded like one Marvin would like. It was a real find. He loved it and we've been eating it ever since. For years we've just called it "The German Dish".

The good news is that you don't need a German/English dictionary to translate "The German Dish". The definition is "delicious" in both languages.

The German Dish

4 slices thick bacon, diced
1 large onion, chopped
2 large potatoes, peeled and diced into 1-inch cubes
16 ounces Polish kielbasa sausage
1 red bell pepper, chopped
1 green bell pepper, chopped
Salt, pepper

In a large skillet, fry bacon until crisp. Remove from pan and drain on paper towels. Add onions to pan, and sauté in bacon drippings until golden brown.

Meanwhile, cook potatoes in slowly boiling water for 10 minutes. Drain and pat dry. Add potatoes to the sautéed onions and cook on low heat for about 10 minutes, stirring often. Add a little olive oil to the pan if the potatoes are sticking.

Prick kielbasa several times with a fork before parboiling in water for 5-10 minutes. Drain. Cut into 1/2 inch slices. Add to onions and potatoes, along with chopped peppers. Cover and cook on low heat for 15 minutes, stirring several times. Season to taste with salt and pepper.

Transfer onto a serving platter and sprinkle with bacon.

Serves 4

To find the best barbeque restaurant, look for a building that should be condemned.

Porky Pig Barbecue

Our family lived in Richmond, Virginia, for five years before we moved to New York in 1979. The reaction by friends and neighbors to our impending move was a universal "Oh, I'm so sorry." Clearly they hated to see us leave, but I think what they were really sorry about was our northern destination.

We got some interesting parting gifts—a flashlight to use during blackouts, warm mittens and hats for the children, and a handmade bracelet with a whistle attached. I was to use the whistle to summon help in case I was mugged. Thankfully I never needed the flashlight or the whistle. The warm mittens and hats really came in handy, however.

The best gift I received, without a doubt, was a recipe for southern barbecue from a neighbor of ours. She gave me a recipe called "Porky Pig Barbecue" to take with me. I owe her big time.

I introduced my new friends in New York to this Southern specialty, and of course they loved it. It goes to show that good barbecue has no regional boundaries.

Porky Pig Barbecue is a vinegar-based barbecue, which has its origins in North Carolina. Other parts of the country strongly debate the merits of their local barbecue. People can be very opinionated about this subject. My opinion? This North Carolina barbecue holds its own against any competitors.

I've shared this recipe with lots of friends over the years. One of my best friends, Anne Zirkle, made this barbecue for her nephew, Wade, after he returned from Iraq.

Wade, a Marine, was injured in Fallujah and airlifted to Germany. One of his first requests was for a barbecue sandwich, which he received. According to Anne, he's a bit of an expert on the subject.

When Wade returned home to Edinburg, Virginia, and tasted the "Porky Pig" version, he smiled and said, "Now that's the way barbecue should taste". That said it all.

Even though there are differences among barbecue aficionados, all agree on three things:

(1) Barbecue is a typically American dish, with roots deeply embedded in the south.
(2) It should be cooked VERY slowly.
(3) To find the best barbecue restaurant, look for a building that should be condemned. The older the building, the better the barbecue.

Thanks to my neighbor in Richmond, we don't need to go in search of great barbecue. It's only as far away as our own kitchen. Just ask Wade Zirkle.

Porky Pig Barbecue

3-4 pound bone-in pork loin roast
1 teaspoon salt
1 teaspoon coarsely ground pepper
2 teaspoons sugar
2 cups vinegar
2-3 dried chipotle peppers*
Your favorite barbeque sauce

Cut fat from the roast. Sprinkle with salt and pepper. Put meat in slow cooker with sugar, vinegar, and peppers. Cook on low heat for 12 hours or until the meat falls from the bone.

Shred meat with a fork. Stir in just enough drippings and your favorite barbecue sauce to moisten meat.

*I added the chipotle peppers (smoked jalapenos) to give more cooking liquid. Leave them out if you like, but you'll be missing some great extra flavor.

Sharpen your knives and enjoy this distinctly Southern treat. Party on!

Mother's Country Ham

Rejoice and be happy, for I'm going to divulge my mother's recipe for one of the most divine foods on earth—country ham. Country ham has no equal. Not even prosciutto, the Italian version of cured ham, comes close.

As soon as fall arrives I begin to crave a good country ham biscuit. There's a chill in the air, Thanksgiving is almost upon us, Christmas is right around the corner, followed by New Year's celebrations and the Super Bowl. Let's face it, there are lots of parties coming up, and as far as I'm concerned, none would be complete without a platter of country ham biscuits on the table.

I practically grew up on country ham. My father was an expert on the subject. He knew exactly how to pick out the best one and would bring it home and hang it in the attic to "cure".

I've never understood the art of picking out a good country ham. I ask the butcher to do it for me and that works fine. I also have no idea why we had them hanging in the attic, but we did.

This delicacy is best enjoyed in moderation. It's loaded with sodium and not too good for those of us with high blood pressure. The key is to slice it VERY thin.

Daddy carved our ham with the precision of a surgeon, using a knife handmade by a neighbor who worked at the Norfolk and Western Railway shops. I'm now the proud owner of "The Knife" and consider it a family heirloom.

Country ham is definitely a Southern thing. Every region has its own brand, and all claim to be the best. Being a native Virginian, I know for a fact that a ham from Smithfield, Virginia, is unbeatable. After all, aren't country hams generally referred to as Smithfield hams? I rest my case.

Mother's recipe is simple and foolproof, as long as you cover the ham tightly so that no steam escapes. Sharpen your knives, and enjoy this distinctly Southern treat. Party on!

Mother's Country Ham

12 – 13 pound country ham
Water
Biscuits or small party rolls

Soak ham in water to cover for at least one day, changing the water several times.

Place a 12-13 pound ham in a roaster* with 7 cups of water. Cover tightly. Place in a cold oven. Turn heat to 500 degrees and cook for 15 minutes. Turn oven off. DO NOT OPEN OVEN DOOR!

After 3 hours, turn on heat to 375 degrees. Cook for 15 minutes. Turn oven off. DON'T OPEN OVEN DOOR. Leave in the oven for 9 hours or overnight. Uncover, and cut off fat layer. Slice the ham VERY thin. Serve on biscuits or small party rolls.

*If you don't have a roaster, place the ham in a large baking dish and seal tightly with foil. I use the bottom of my broiler pan, which works great.

Directions for Cooking ½ Ham

Follow the same procedure for cooking 1/2 ham (6-7 pounds), except add only 3 cups of water, and cut the initial cooking time to 10 minutes. Wait only 1 1/2 hours between baking periods instead of 3 hours. Leave in the oven for 5 hours.

POULTRY AND SEAFOOD

Uncle John and Aunt Ruby
The only thing missing from the picture is a pitchfork.

Sunday Dinner Roast Chicken

I remember as a child visiting the farm in Crewe, Virginia, where my father grew up. My grandma lived there with my Uncle John and Aunt Ruby in the old family home, about three miles outside of town.

Uncle John's farm was complete with a barn, a spring, a small creek, pigs, chickens, and a white mule named Pete. In this rural area there wasn't much to do, so I had to make my own entertainment. I learned how to gather eggs and slop the hogs. I remember catching crawfish in the creek, riding Pete bareback, and having watermelon seed spitting contests with my cousins.

I especially remember Aunt Ruby. She was a plump, pleasant woman with a pronounced Southern accent. I never saw her without an apron over her dress. She busied herself all day in the kitchen and by dinnertime the table was overflowing with an amazing variety of her down-home cooking. It was something to behold.

A roast chicken dinner was the most memorable for me. That morning, to my horror, I watched Aunt Ruby walk across the yard to the chicken coop, come out holding a chicken by the neck, and very matter-of-factly lay it down on a tree stump and cut off its head with a hatchet. The chicken then did what I'd always heard about - it ran around the yard like a chicken with its head cut off! When the chicken finally stopped, Aunt Ruby took it into the kitchen and covered it with boiling water before plucking the feathers out.

That's the last I saw of that hen until it appeared on the dining room table that night, browned and crisp on the outside, juicy and tender on the inside. It was the perfect roast chicken.

I've been in search of a recipe for years to replicate it, and I finally found one in a newspaper clipping Mother had saved. This roast chicken is a lot fancier than Aunt Ruby would have made, but the results are similar. Aunt Ruby probably would have served this wonderful chicken for Sunday dinner after church.

Even though it's not fresh from the hen house, I'm pretty sure Aunt Ruby would love it anyway. At least there's no hatchet and bloodshed involved in this version!

Sunday Dinner Roast Chicken

Large roasting chicken (about 3-4 pounds)
1/2 cup of finely chopped fresh herbs (I use parsley, thyme, basil, and chives)
Salt, pepper
1/4 cup olive oil
1 lemon, cut in half
3 sprigs fresh rosemary

Place a baking dish into a cold oven. Heat to 450 degrees. Wash chicken inside and out and pat dry. Gently separate the skin from the breast meat on both sides by sliding your fingers under the skin. Push the chopped herbs into these gaps. Drizzle a little olive oil over the herbs. Pull skin back into place.

Sprinkle the cavity of the chicken with salt and pepper. Then stuff the cavity with lemon and rosemary. Tuck the wings under the bird and tie with kitchen twine. Also use kitchen twine to tie the legs together. Rub a little olive oil over the skin of the chicken and sprinkle with salt and pepper.

Remove the hot baking dish from the oven and add a little oil. Put the chicken on one side, breast side down on the dish and put into the oven. Cook for 5 minutes, turn the chicken over on the other side, breast side down, and cook for another 5 minutes. After browning the breasts on both sides, turn the chicken over on its back. Reduce heat to 425 degrees and bake for 1 hour. Remove from oven. Allow to sit for at least 10 minutes before serving.

Serves 6

The UN-happy camper at Brownie Scout Camp—1950
It was poison ivy, mosquitoes, chiggers, snakes, raccoons, and the latrine she didn't like.

Grilled Lemon Chicken

I like camping—in theory, that is. The idea of communing with nature is really appealing. I love the thought of cooking over an open fire, sleeping under the stars, hiking along beautiful trails, and fishing in a pristine lake. It's the poison ivy, mosquitoes, chiggers, mud, mildew, snakes, raccoons, and the latrine that I don't like. It's not that I haven't tried to like it. After all, as a child I went to Girl Scout camp, church camp, Future Homemakers of America camp, and nature camp.

Nature camp was the most memorable. When I was in the seventh grade, my mother's garden club, the Spade and Trowel Garden Club in Roanoke sponsored me as their "summer camper". It was supposed to be quite the place to become environmentally aware and to commune with nature.

In addition to taking classes and keeping a notebook, we were required to take bird walks. This dreaded activity meant getting up before dawn and walking through the woods making a list of birdcalls we heard, none of which I remember.

On the positive side, nature camp was co-ed. The boys were cute, and I liked the evening campfires and enjoying such delicacies as "s'mores" and, believe it or not, copperhead snake "steaks". The counselors actually killed the snakes and cooked them over the campfire. That delicate white meat was quite tasty. It was an early culinary experience that I'll never forget.

Even though I'm all grown up now, I still consider myself a camper wannabe. I'm always attracted to recipes that sound like they could be cooked out in the woods and still be fabulous. A friend's recipe for grilled lemon chicken was the perfect match. If it could be grilled at home, why not on a portable gas grill in the woods?

I tried the recipe (at home, thank you very much) and loved it. The chicken was juicy and delicious, with wonderful lemon and herb flavors.

This favorite has never failed to elicit rave reviews. I can highly recommend it, even if you choose to cook it in the woods. The mosquitoes, chiggers, snakes, and raccoons are waiting for you there.

Grilled Lemon Chicken*

1/2 cup fresh lemon juice
1/4 cup vegetable oil
1 teaspoon salt
1/2 teaspoon garlic salt
1/4 teaspoon pepper
1/2 teaspoon dried basil
1/2 teaspoon dried marjoram
4 split chicken breasts, skin on

Combine lemon juice, oil, salt, pepper, and spices. Pour over chicken. Let sit for at least an hour, spooning mixture over chicken several times.

Cook on the grill until crispy and browned, brushing with marinade and turning as needed.

*If you're actually going camping, put the chicken and marinade together in a zip top bag, and store it in your cooler until ready to cook on the grill.

Serves 4

Rule Number One
Never let an 8-year-old pound the chicken for this dish. *

Chicken Cordon Bleu

A favorite "stand-by" dinner at our house is Chicken Cordon Bleu. It sounds fancy but it's nothing more than chicken, ham, and cheese that's layered, folded up, and baked. Our kids grew up loving this dish.

When new neighbors from Germany moved in across the street from us in New York, I invited them to dinner. I served Chicken Cordon Bleu to Elke and Wolfgang Karsten and their two young daughters, Christiane and Sabine. Right away, Chicken Cordon Bleu became a favorite in their house, too.

We were neighbors for fewer than two years before they moved back to Germany. Their older daughter, Christiane, came back to visit us the following year. She and our daughter Whitney had a great time together. I made sure to fix Chicken Cordon Bleu for Christiane so she would feel at home, which she did.

During her visit, I introduced Christiane to another of our dinner favorites called "Clean Out the Refrigerator Night". This was an opportunity to get rid of all of those little half dishes of leftover things (hopefully without mold on them), clogging up the refrigerator shelves. We'd end up with lots of mismatched meats and vegetables, but nobody seemed to care. Basically, it's a gastronomic free for all.

I laid all of the leftovers out on the counter, and everybody got to choose what they wanted. Whoever came first to dinner got to be first in line. No one was ever late to dinner on those nights.

This concept was a real novelty for Christiane, who had never heard of such a thing. When she returned home, she asked to have a "Clean Out the Refrigerator Night". I don't think this translates into German very well. Elke had no clue.

A couple of years later our son Blake visited the Karstens in Germany. He had a great time experiencing lots of new people, places, and things. Elke made Chicken Cordon Bleu for him so he would feel at home, which he did.

It turns out that Chicken Cordon Bleu was the common denominator that made two kids far away from their families feel right at home. It'll make you feel good, too. Try it and see. Your family will love it, and the leftovers will be a big hit at your next "Clean Out the Refrigerator Night."

Chicken Cordon Bleu

1 pound boneless, skinless chicken breasts
¼ lb. Black Forest ham, sliced thin**
¼ lb. Swiss cheese, sliced thin
Salt, pepper
Garlic powder (optional)
1/3 cup canned breadcrumbs
1 teaspoon oil
Fresh parsley, chopped

Lay chicken breasts flat. Sprinkle with salt, pepper and garlic powder. Divide ham and cheese into equal portions. On half of each chicken breast, layer cheese, ham, and top with more cheese. Fold the other half of the chicken over to form a packet.

Mix the breadcrumbs and oil until well blended. Pour onto a flat plate. Press the chicken packets into the breadcrumbs, coating well. Place the chicken packets onto a non-greased baking sheet. Bake for 30 minutes in a 350 degree oven.

Garnish with parsley and serve.

**I like to substitute prosciutto for the ham. I've also substituted thinly sliced country ham. Both of these add more flavor than regular ham.

Serves 2

* The eight-year-old pounding the chicken is our granddaughter, Sydney Smith.

Sydney Smith, future Food Network Star
"Okay, I've got the oven. Now give me the recipe for the "Gourmet" Chicken Breasts. Pronto!"

Jerrie's "Gourmet" Chicken Breasts

Every cook has to begin somewhere—whether it's in early childhood with a toy oven cooking tiny cupcakes by the heat of a light bulb, when you first leave home and begin to fend for yourself in the real world, or as a newlywed just learning your way around the kitchen.

I never set foot in the kitchen until after I was married, although my friend Anne claims that I used to make hot chocolate and grilled cheese sandwiches when we were kids. Quite honestly, the only thing I remember cooking was marshmallows over a campfire.

Because I really can relate to the novice cook, just know that I feel your pain and I'm here to help. This one's for you. This dish is so simple that I promise anybody can make it, probably even the kid with the toy oven.

The recipe is for chicken breasts baked in a sauce of brown gravy and apricot preserves with a dash of cloves. That's it—nothing fancy but it looks impressive and tastes great.

A good friend of ours, Jerrie Frye, gave me this recipe decades ago. We've both gotten A LOT of mileage out of this dish. She has entertained her husband's customers in their home quite a few times over the years and got the hang of pulling off a business dinner with sometimes very short notice. The key to her success is simplicity.

According to Jerrie, she created this recipe after having attended a dinner party where the hostess served Cornish game hens with a delicious gravy and wild rice with water chestnuts. Jerrie got the recipe and revised it by substituting chicken breasts for the game hens, a box of Uncle Ben's wild rice for the real thing, and toasted pecans for the water chestnuts. I think the result is pure genius.

The secret to this recipe is the gravy. That's what propels it from ordinary to the "gourmet" category. It seems impossible that four ingredients could taste so good, but they do.

If you'd like to throw your first dinner party, follow Jerrie's lead and keep it simple. Serve this dish with boxed rice, a premade salad, and a store-bought cake. Hide all of the evidence and take credit for this delicious meal. Now, doesn't that feel good?

Jerrie's "Gourmet" Chicken Breasts

2 skinless boneless chicken breasts
1 package brown gravy mix (1 ounce)
1/2 cup water
1/2 cup apricot preserves*
Dash of ground cloves

Combine brown gravy mix with water and stir until smooth. Add apricot preserves. In a small saucepan, heat on medium and stir until the gravy comes to a mild boil. Pour over chicken breasts placed in a baking dish. Cover and bake at 350 degrees for 30 minutes. Uncover and continue baking for 15 minutes. Plate, and pour gravy over the chicken.

Serves 2

*I've substituted hot pepper jelly for the apricot preserves, which adds a little extra "zip" to the gravy.

To Sop or Not To Sop—That is the Question
Daddy wasn't finished eating until his plate was cleaned with a piece of Merita bread

Drunk Chicken

To sop or not to sop—that is the question. Some say yes. Some say no. I say absolutely! I say yes because the best part of the meal is often left on the plate: the au jus gravy from a nice prime rib dinner, for example. Who could possibly want to leave that behind? Take a piece of bread (a small one, thank you), sop it in the gravy, and taste the goodness. Once you start, you'll never look back.

Speaking of prime rib and au jus gravy, isn't that what a French dip sandwich is all about? Another good example of mainstream sopping is dipping bread into flavored olive oils. Everybody knows that the good stuff is at the bottom of the dish, and we can't wait to soak it up.

I learned the art of sopping from my father. His dinner wasn't finished until his plate had been meticulously cleaned with a nice piece of Merita bread. Nothing ever went to waste with him. No matter what was for dinner, he sopped the leftovers with gusto. My mother just rolled her eyes and pretended not to notice.

I've happily carried on my father's tradition of sopping. My husband just rolls his eyes and pretends not to notice. One of my favorites is to clean the leftover Balsamic vinegar at the bottom of my salad bowl with crusty bread. It's delicious. Don't knock it until you've tried it.

The best thing I've ever sopped was the flavorful juice left over from a meal in New York City. I remember sitting in the courtyard of Barbella restaurant on a beautiful spring day having lunch with a friend. I ordered the special of the day, which was a pan-seared rabbit, cooked in red wine, mushrooms and onions. It was exquisite. Not only was it one of the best meals I've ever eaten, but the leftovers, sopped with a piece of warm bread, were indescribably good.

That fantastic meal can never be reproduced, but it can be copied. The closest I can come to this heavenly experience is a dish we love at our house called Coq au Vin. When translated, it means chicken in red wine. It also has bourbon, bacon, mushrooms and onions in it.

Because of all the alcohol that goes into this dish, we renamed it "Drunk Chicken". The alcohol cooks away, leaving a delicious flavor that permeates everything. The essence that remains on your plate is a sopper's dream come true. Grab a piece of bread and have a go at it.

Just know that my father is smiling down at you while you're doing this. My mother is rolling her eyes. Pay no attention to her.

Drunk Chicken*

6 slices of bacon, diced
2 tablespoons butter
4 large split chicken breasts, skin left on
Salt, pepper
½ cup sliced onions
1 cup sliced fresh mushrooms
2 garlic cloves, minced
15 ounce jar pearl onions
1 large can button mushrooms
2 tablespoons flour
¼ cup bourbon
2 cups Burgundy wine
¼ cup chopped fresh parsley
1 bay leaf
¼ teaspoon thyme
Chopped parsley for garnish

Brown bacon in large skillet and set aside. Add butter to bacon drippings. Season chicken with salt and pepper and brown on both sides in the skillet. Remove chicken and put in a large casserole dish. Add sliced onions, sliced fresh mushrooms, and garlic to skillet and brown. Remove and put in the casserole dish, along with the jarred onions and canned mushrooms.

Stir flour into grease in skillet. Pour in bourbon and wine and bring to a boil, stirring constantly. Cook for a few minutes until it begins to thicken. Pour over ingredients in the casserole dish. Sprinkle with chopped parsley, bay leaf, thyme, and bacon. Cook in a 400-degree oven for 1 1/4 hours, uncovered. Garnish with more chopped parsley, and serve with rice.

*Be sure to serve with crusty rolls or bread for sopping your plate.

Serves 4

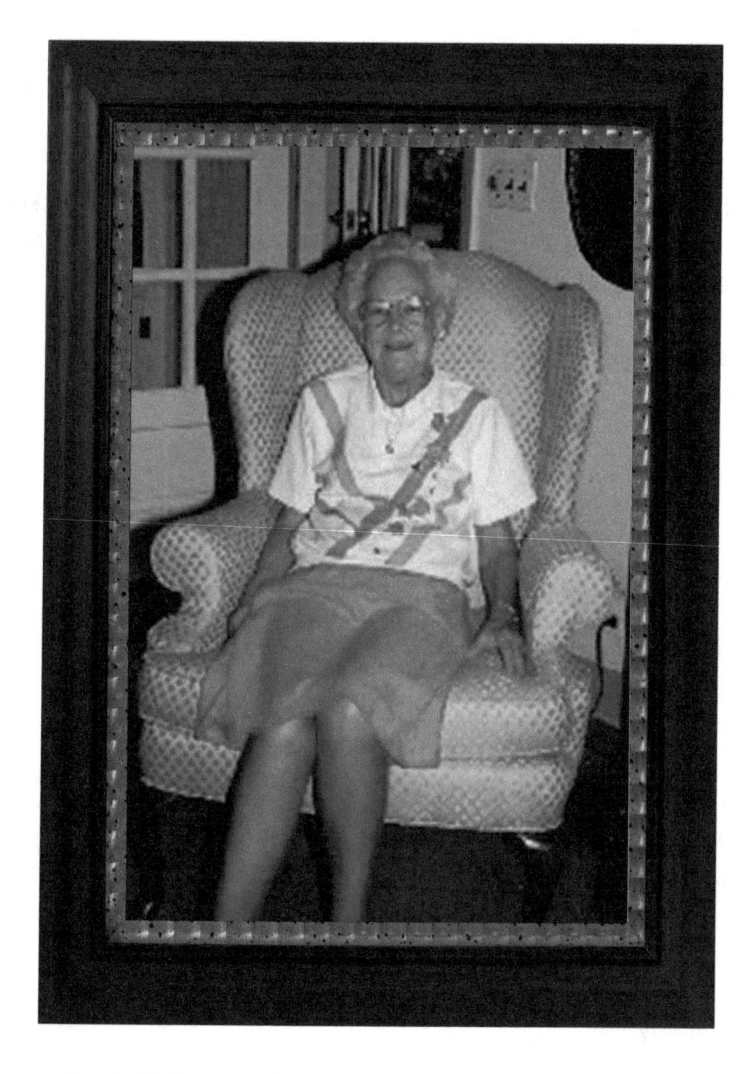

Dottie Walton – The "Queen of the Chicken Casserole"
In order to be a good Baptist, you need to have a decent casserole recipe.

Dottie's Famous Chicken Casserole

I'm convinced that one of the greatest inventions in the history of cooking (aside from the discovery of fire) has to be the casserole. You can combine just about any variety of ingredients, mix with a sauce of some sort, add a topping, bake, and voila! You've got a casserole.

I'm a big fan of casseroles and have been since I was a kid. I was practically raised on them. After all, my father was a Baptist minister. I know all about covered dish dinners at church, where casseroles were king. I was convinced that in order to be a good Baptist, you had to have a good casserole recipe.

I remember Daddy telling a joke about this very topic. I must have been in elementary school at the time. It was considered to be a real "knee slapper" back then. It seems that a teacher asked her students to bring a symbol of their religion to class for show and tell. The next day the Catholic kid brought a rosary, the Jewish kid brought a menorah, and the Baptist kid brought a casserole. I can certainly relate to that.

I've probably eaten every kind of casserole ever invented, so I feel I'm fully qualified as an expert on this subject. One of my favorite casserole recipes is one that I got from a good friend in New York, Dottie Walton. Dottie was a lovely person whose happy nature was infectious. I'm smiling now just thinking about her.

Dottie was a member of P.E.O., an international sisterhood that promotes education for women through scholarships. It's a wonderful organization, and I was fortunate to be invited to join her chapter in Tarrytown, New York. We met in the evening and periodically had dinner meetings.

Whenever Dottie was the hostess, she served her chicken casserole, which we LOVED. We started calling it "Dottie's Famous Chicken Casserole," and begged for the recipe. When she gave it to us, we were amazed at how few ingredients there were, and how simple it was to make.

Dottie gave the recipe to me, and it's my pleasure to pass it on to you. You don't even have to be Baptist to love it!

Dottie's Famous Chicken Casserole

8 split chicken breasts (skin on, on the bone)*
2 cans cream of chicken soup
1 pint sour cream
8 ounce package Pepperidge Farm herb dressing
1 cup chicken broth
1 stick butter

Place chicken breasts in baking dish, skin side up, and cook for 1 hour at 350 degrees, uncovered. Remove from oven, and let cool. Remove the skin and bones, and cut chicken into bite-size pieces. Combine soup and sour cream. Add chicken to mixture. Pour into baking dish.

Mix dressing, chicken broth, and butter together. Sprinkle over top of chicken. Bake for 30 minutes at 350 degrees. Let set for a few minutes before serving.

*I use split chicken breasts because chicken cooked on the bone with the skin on is juicier and more flavorful than skinless, boneless breasts. I make sure that the casserole mixture has lots of chicken in it, otherwise it will be runny. You can easily double or triple this recipe. Make it a day in advance if you like and refrigerate it. It keeps well.

Serves 6-8

Joy fishing in Bedford County, Virginia—1956
Giving her a long stick instead of a fishing rod was her mother's idea.

Oven Fried Crunchy Catfish

My father instilled a love of fishing in me when I was a little girl. I've been catching worms, baiting my own hook, and casting my line into the water for as long as I can remember. Early on Daddy taught me the two most important rules of fishing—silence and patience.

My first big moment to show off my fishing expertise came when I was old enough to participate in the annual fishing derby for kids in my hometown of Roanoke, Virginia. A small pond at a local park was stocked for this event every year.

Early on a spring Saturday morning young Roanoke fishermen descended on this park armed with all sorts of fishing gear. We stood elbow to elbow around the pond and, at the sound of a whistle, cast our lines into the water. We were neither silent nor patient.

What followed was utter chaos. Lines got tangled, kids slipped on the bank, and premature shouts of "I've got one!" filled the air. Miraculously some fish were caught during this event. The winners got a certificate and their names printed in the paper. It was a big deal.

Daddy not only taught me the virtues of being quiet and patient when fishing, he showed me how far out to cast, the right amount of weight to use, that bait could be anything that wiggled on a hook, and not to jerk my line until the bobber went all the way under the water. He even gave me my own tackle box.

I'm happy to say that our son Blake inherited the fishing gene. When he was little, Daddy took him fishing. I remember the first time they fished together. I watched as the two of them walked down the street toward the pond in our neighborhood. They were carrying fishing rods, a bucket, and a well-worn tackle box.

My knowledge of fishing ended after cleaning them. My mother took over after that. Mother cooked fish the good old Southern way—rolled in cornmeal and fried. They taste great that way but aren't very good for us.

Happily, I now know what to do with fish after I've cleaned them. It's pretty easy. I use a recipe for oven-fried fish that's healthy and delicious.

It's the next best thing I've found to eating Southern fried fish at my mother's dinner table. I think you'll like it too, even if it is good for you.

Oven Fried Crunchy Catfish

2 large catfish fillets
1 egg, beaten
2 tablespoons milk
2 cups crushed low fat Salt and Vinegar potato chips*
Cooking spray
Lemon wedges

In a large bowl beat egg. Add milk. Stir until combined. Crush potato chips into small pieces and place on a large flat plate. Dip catfish fillets in the egg mixture and then press into the crushed potato chips. The fillet should be thoroughly coated on both sides with crushed chips.

Place catfish on a baking sheet sprayed with cooking oil. Then spray the fillets lightly with additional cooking oil and bake at 400 degrees for 20 minutes on the lower shelf of your oven.

Sprinkle liberally with fresh lemon juice and serve with lemon wedges.

*Serve the rest of the bag of chips as a side dish. They are, after all, potatoes.

Serves 2

Uncle Milton and Aunt Rena—1958
The huge silver fish hung in the air momentarily, and then it was gone.

The Swordfish Steak That Didn't Get Away

Fishermen always like to talk about "the one that got away". It's usually an exaggerated and detailed story about the monster they "almost" caught. Well, I'm one of those people. Let me tell you right up front that I'm passionate about a number of things in my life. Fishing happens to be one of them. I actually know a fair amount about this subject.

Using the right bait was the first lesson my father taught me about fishing. He used worms. Because we had a compost pile in the corner of our backyard, I was never at a loss for worms. Lizards were also good bait.

As kids, Loulie Johnston and I caught lizards in the woods near her family's summer cabin. We set up a little bait stand at the end of the driveway and sold them for three cents apiece, or two for five cents. Sometimes the bait business was brisk. After all, who could resist two cute little girls sitting on crates by the side of the road selling lizards?

I learned deep water fishing techniques from my Uncle Milton. He and Aunt Rena lived on the Chesapeake Bay in Maryland. When my family vacationed there, I spent lots of time fishing on his boat.

Uncle Milton taught me how to chum. He took a bucket of fish heads and miscellaneous bloody parts of God knows what and threw it overboard. We slowly chugged through it over and over again. Big fish were attracted to the carnage and went into a feeding frenzy. Chumming wasn't a favorite of mine because, quite honestly, it smelled terrible. Stinky, yes, but it was highly successful.

Another lesson I learned from Uncle Milton was to follow the birds to the best fishing spot. Whenever we saw lots of gulls circling and diving, we could be sure that they had found a school of fish. The birds were never wrong.

As with any activity one loves, there are highlights and lowlights. As for the lowlights, it's hard to choose between the massive dose of chiggers and poison ivy I got while lake fishing and the time my cousin's wife, Gina, threw up on me while we were on a deep sea fishing trip. I guess I'd choose the latter, because it was my idea to go, even though the seas were rough and the weather forecast grim. This happened in the 1970s; I still haven't heard the end of it.

On the other hand, the highlight of my fishing career took place while we vacationed in Hawaii. I opted to go fishing on a professional fishing boat geared to catch really big fish. It was a beautiful day. Little flying fish swam along beside us, and rainbows arched above us.

The captain strapped me into a chair and gave me a huge fishing pole, which fit into a sturdy holder in front of me. I was so excited! As we headed farther out into the Pacific Ocean, my pole suddenly bent down and I held onto it for dear life. Out of the water came a huge silver fish with an incredible fin and a long snout. It hung in the air momentarily, glistening in the sun, and then it was gone. I had snagged a swordfish. It was the one that got away from me. Even though I didn't reel him in, I was thrilled to have had that one moment in time. I'll never forget it.

I don't have a stuffed swordfish on my wall, but I do have an excellent recipe for swordfish. Whenever I prepare this dish, I pretend it's the one I almost caught. This one won't get away, however.

The Swordfish Steak That Didn't Get Away

2 swordfish steaks, 1 inch thick
4 cloves garlic, crushed
¼ cup fresh ginger, peeled and sliced
8 peppercorns
½ cup rice wine vinegar
½ cup soy sauce
1 cup white wine
6 tablespoons cold butter
Olive oil
Salt, pepper

Put garlic, ginger, peppercorns, vinegar, soy sauce, and wine into the blender to make the sauce. Blend well. Pour mixture into a small saucepan, and add the butter. Bring to a boil, and cook until it's reduced in half. Strain and keep warm.

Make sure the racks on your grill are clean. Preheat the grill. Rub a little olive oil on the swordfish steaks and sprinkle with salt and pepper. Grill over high heat for 4-5 minutes. The steaks should be nicely browned. Carefully turn the fish over and cook for another 3-4 minutes. Don't overcook, or it can become too dry.

Serve at once, with the sauce poured over it.

Serves 2

Blake showing off his clean "Willie Stargell" Ball—1980
Like an idiot, I traded the real autographed ball for another one just to shut him up.

Winterset Shrimp Scampi

My most dreaded date on my children's New York school calendar was the mid-winter vacation. It was a week off in the middle of February that struck fear into the heart of even the most creative parent. It was too cold for the children to play outside, and being cooped up inside with active kids for seven days was lunacy.

The obvious answer was to abandon ship and hit the road, which we did every year. By the time they graduated from high school, we were well traveled.

Our most memorable trip was to Florida in 1980. I took the children, five-year-old Whitney and seven-year-old Blake, to visit my parents. Mother and Daddy spent the winter months at a lovely trailer park in their Airstream travel trailer. The park, named Winterset, was a serene place where adults could relax and enjoy a carefree winter. Enter the Smiths.........

Upon our arrival, Whitney's eyes lit up when she saw the swimming pool. Before we could stop her, she jumped in the deep end and sank like a stone. I went in after her, still clad in boots, sweater, and a skirt, and pulled her out. She was fine, thought it was fun, and wanted to do it again.

The next day Daddy and I took Blake to a spring training baseball game between the Pittsburg Pirates and the Detroit Tigers. We sat behind first base and watched Willie Stargell play. After the game I bought a ball signed by this baseball legend for Blake.

At the sight of the autographed ball, Blake threw a world-class tantrum because it was "dirty" with ink on it. Like an idiot, I traded the Willie Stargell ball for a "clean" one, just to shut Blake up. I still can't believe I did that, but as the old saying goes, "desperate people do desperate things".

In the days to follow, the children discovered that picking oranges from the trees, playing hopscotch on the shuffleboard courts, and riding bikes too fast were frowned upon at Winterset.

All wasn't lost that week, however. We did spend a wonderful day at Disney World and another at the beach. The kids learned a lot about camping and trailer life and enjoyed quality time with their grandparents.

We ate really well during our visit. The children learned that their granny could turn out top-notch meals using nothing more than a couple of gas burners in the trailer and a charcoal grill outside. Now THAT takes talent.

The night before we left, Mother fixed shrimp scampi. She bought fresh shrimp for this dish. The only shrimp I had seen before were in the grocery store on ice looking clean, pretty, and pink. These hideous looking gray creatures had heads, bug eyes, and antenna. Sometimes it's just better not to see what you eat in its natural state. Despite the shock of seeing the "before" version of dinner, the end result was wonderful. It was one of the best meals I have eaten.

The next day we flew home to New York, and Winterset returned to normal – a nice serene place where adults could relax and spend a carefree winter.

I hope you'll enjoy the recipe I use for shrimp scampi. This dinner is especially good when eaten on a February night in Florida under fragrant orange trees with those you love.

Winterset Shrimp Scampi

½ cup extra virgin olive oil
4 large cloves garlic, cut into slivers
2 pounds large shrimp (20-30 per pound), peeled, deveined, and patted dry
Sea salt and freshly ground pepper
¼ cup finely chopped fresh parsley
Juice of 1 lemon

In a large skillet, brown garlic in olive oil over low heat until it turns golden brown. This will take a few minutes. Raise the heat to medium high and add the shrimp. Sprinkle with a generous pinch of salt and pepper to taste. Cook the shrimp until it turns pink on the bottom side. Turn it over, add the parsley, and cook until the shrimp is done (about 2 minutes more). Add fresh lemon juice to the skillet and stir for another 30 seconds. Remove shrimp to a serving platter and serve immediately.

Serves 4

PASTA

Joy (age 6) with her father
It was a cold, blustery day, but I didn't care. We were taking Thanksgiving to people!

The Great Macaroni Dish

I was probably about six years old when my father took me with him to deliver Thanksgiving dinners to people who couldn't afford them. It was the day before Thanksgiving and, now that I think about it, Mother was busy cooking and probably asked him to take me along just to get me out of her way.

Our church had donated turkey dinners, with all the trimmings, for needy families in town. I was excited to go along on such an important mission with Daddy. With a carload of boxes and turkeys, we headed off to take Thanksgiving to those who otherwise wouldn't have one.

Most of these families lived in a section of town that might as well have been a foreign country to me. The houses were small and run down, the yards were barren, and dark coal smoke rose from their chimneys.

Daddy parked the car and we began to go door to door with our bounty. I'll never forget the smiles of happiness on the people's faces in those shabby houses when we gave them their dinners.

It was a cold, blustery day and dogs barked at us, but I didn't care. We were bringing Thanksgiving to people! It felt great.

I don't think Mother and Daddy ever realized how that day changed my life. I learned the joy of giving. No Sunday school lesson could have been more effective.

I've carried that lesson with me through my life and have found great satisfaction in it. I've been involved in lots of outreach activities over the years, but one event in particular stands out in my mind. It had to do with a soup kitchen.

After hearing a woman speak about our local soup kitchen, I was moved by her poignant stories and impulsively volunteered to serve a meal there. Immediately I realized I had volunteered to feed 60-70 people lunch without any idea what I was doing. Desperate, I ran home and searched through my cookbooks for a dish that was easy, satisfying, and could be stretched to serve an army. I found a macaroni recipe that was perfect for the occasion.

Several of my adventurous friends pitched in to help chop, slice, dice, cook, and serve a meal to the masses. It was fun. As we served lunch that day I was touched by the smiles of gratitude and the occasional "God Bless You" from those going through the line.

I had experienced this feeling somewhere before. I'm pretty sure it was on a cold November day long ago when a little girl went with her Daddy to share Thanksgiving with needy people. It felt great.

The Great Macaroni Dish

1½ pounds lean ground beef
1 cup chopped onions
1 large green pepper, chopped
1 tablespoon chili powder
2 cloves garlic, minced
2 cups beef gravy (I use the canned variety)
15 ½ oz. can kidney beans, drained
2 cups cooked macaroni
¼ teaspoon salt
¼ teaspoon pepper
1 cup shredded cheddar cheese (Add more if you like)

Brown the ground beef. Add the onions, green pepper, chili powder, and garlic and stir until the vegetables are tender. Add the gravy, beans, macaroni, salt, and pepper and stir until combined. Pour the mixture into a 2 quart baking dish (12x8x2 inches) and bake at 450 degrees for 15 minutes. Stir it, top with cheese, and bake until the cheese melts.

Serves 8-10

The smiling hairnet-clad cafeteria ladies were happy to serve us anything we wanted.

S&W Cafeteria's Macaroni and Cheese

My family rarely ate out when I was growing up in the 1950s in Roanoke, Virginia. My friends didn't either. Our mothers fixed nice wholesome meals at home. That's just the way it was.

At my house we gathered around the dinner table promptly at 6:00, said the blessing, and had family discussions while we ate. We had to eat our vegetables to get dessert and wait to be excused from the table when we were finished. There were no distractions. It was good, quality family time.

When we did go out, it was a big deal. The destination was always the same—the S&W Cafeteria downtown. The S&W was known for good, inexpensive, authentic Southern cooking. There was something for everybody, even for the one picky eater in every family—me.

Going through the glitzy cafeteria line was an exciting experience for a kid not used to so many choices for dinner. Standing on my tiptoes, seeing all the food under glistening lights, was a bit overwhelming. The smiling, hairnet-clad cafeteria ladies were happy to serve us anything we wanted.

Despite the opportunities, I was predictable. At the end of the line, I always had the same items –fried chicken, macaroni and cheese, chocolate pudding, and chocolate milk. My favorite, by far, was the macaroni and cheese, luscious and creamy.

In addition to their food, the S&W was known for its "Family Night", a brilliant marketing tool. Every Thursday night the restaurant showed cartoons upstairs for the children, free of charge. While our parents enjoyed some quiet time together, we rushed up to the mezzanine after dinner to be entertained by Mickey Mouse, Donald Duck, and Bugs Bunny. While the projectionist changed reels or spliced broken film, we honed our shadow puppet skills on the blank movie screen.

My last memories of the S&W were from my high school days. I was a cheerleader, and before our Friday night games, our squad ate there. After dinner, we rode in a convertible to nearby Victory Stadium, waving and cheering. Even though I was in high school, I still ordered the same dinner, especially the macaroni and cheese. Some things never change.

Even though the S&W cafeteria is a faded piece of Roanoke history, I'm richer for having been a part of it. The lasting legacy I have from it is an unwavering love for macaroni and cheese, which I consider one of the best comfort foods on earth.

Good macaroni and cheese is decadent and rich with flavor. It has absolutely nothing to do with the horrible notion of boxed noodles and tasteless powdered cheese. It has everything to do with the S&W Cafeteria version – luscious and creamy.

My recipe is great, if I don't mind saying so myself. It would be perfect for a little girl standing on her tiptoes, gazing under glistening cafeteria lights, choosing her favorite food for dinner. She'd choose this one for sure.

S&W Cafeteria's Macaroni and Cheese

8 oz. elbow macaroni
1/2 cup of reserved cooking water
1/2 stick butter
3 tablespoons. flour
2 1/2 cups milk
1/2 lb. (8 ounces) grated extra sharp cheddar cheese
1/4 cup grated Asiago cheese
1 teaspoon salt
1/4 teaspoon pepper

Topping

1/4 stick melted butter
1 cup Panko breadcrumbs
3/4 cup grated extra sharp cheddar cheese
1/4 cup grated Asiago cheese

Mix ingredients together and sprinkle over cooled macaroni and cheese before baking.

Cook macaroni in boiling water until done. Drain, reserving ½ cup of the cooking water. Put drained macaroni and water in a large bowl. Melt butter in saucepan. Add flour and wisk until smooth. Add milk gradually and stir until the mixture comes to the boiling point. Add cheese, salt, and pepper, and wisk until well blended. Combine cheese sauce with macaroni. Pour into a medium casserole dish and let cool. Top with breadcrumb mixture and bake for 20 minutes at 400 degrees.

Serve 6-8

Aunt Rena and Uncle Milton – 1953
Aunt Rena's lasagna recipe stood the test of time. So did Aunt Rena. She lived to be 104.

Aunt Rena's Lasagna

In addition to swapping stories at a family reunion, or browsing through old photo albums, I think that family recipes can also bring back fond memories of the past. They are, without a doubt, revisiting a piece of family history that can be passed from one generation to the next. If you're lucky, you have some handwritten ones like I do, making them even more special.

For me, recreating these recipes evokes some great childhood memories. My Aunt Rena's lasagna is a perfect example.

Aunt Rena and Uncle Milton had a home on the Chesapeake Bay in Cape Anne, Maryland, which was a natural family gathering place in the summer. I always looked forward to "going to the bay" for vacation. It was a chance to go fishing, swimming, crabbing, and run barefoot with my cousins. I loved it.

Aunt Rena dealt with the influx of summer company somehow. She made it look easy, as a matter of fact. If we caught fish, we cleaned them, and she cooked them. If we caught crabs, she steamed them, and we ate them at the newspaper-covered picnic table.

Dinner was served on the big screened-in porch after a day of fun and sun. Believe me, lots of funny stories were shared around that dinner table, as well as some great food.

Aunt Rena's lasagna was a family favorite and has definitely stood the test of time. So did Aunt Rena. She lived to be 104.

At her 100th birthday party I asked if she minded my writing about her and sharing her recipe with my readers. Obviously she agreed to it because here it is. I like to think that she's smiling down on us as we make her lasagna, happy that her recipe lives on.

Aunt Rena's Lasagna*

Meat Sauce:
1 1/2 lbs. hamburger
1 teaspoon garlic salt
1/2 teaspoon oregano
1 1/2 teaspoons salt
1 lb. can or 2 cups tomatoes
2 (6 oz.) cans tomato paste

Brown meat, spoon off fat. Add remaining ingredients. Simmer uncovered 1/2 hour. Stir now and then.

Cheese Filling:
3 cups cottage cheese
1/2 cup Parmesan cheese
2 teaspoons parsley flakes
2 beaten eggs
2 teaspoons salt
1/2 teaspoon pepper
1 lb. mozzarella cheese, grated

Mix together above ingredients.

Lasagna Noodles:

Cook 12 lasagna noodles until tender (about 20 minutes) in large amount of boiling salted water. Drain. Rinse with cold water. Place half the noodles in a 13 x 9 x 2 inch baking pan. Spread half of the cheese filling over the noodles. Cover with half of the meat sauce. Repeat layers. Sprinkle some Parmesan cheese on top.

Bake at 375 degrees for 30 minutes. Let stand for at least 10 minutes before cutting into squares.

Serves 12

*I've written this recipe exactly the way it appears on Aunt Rena's recipe card. I'm guessing that this recipe dates back to the 1950s, maybe earlier. I would change only a few things to update her lasagna. First, I would substitute lean ground beef for the "hamburger" she has listed, and I would use low fat ricotta cheese instead of cottage cheese. I would also add 1 teaspoon each of basil and oregano and eliminate the salt.

**Aunt Rena's Lasagna has smaller portions than today's version. When divided into twelve servings, each piece would be about three inches square. An order of lasagna at most restaurants today would be at least twice that big. Maybe that's the reason a lot of Americans are getting bigger, too. It's food for thought.

Joy, Marvin, and Lois—2001
We will never forget the warmth around her table on that cold January night.

Lois's White Bean and Sausage Rigatoni

For several years in the mid-to-late 90s, my husband Marvin and I drove once a month from Sleepy Hollow, New York, to Roanoke, Virginia, to visit my mother and to take care of his parents. It was 1,000 miles round trip and took us 8 ½ hours each way.

During that four-day weekend trip, we not only checked on my mother, who was in a nursing home, but worked hard at Marvin's parents' house to help them remain independent in their home.

While there, the house was cleaned, the laundry done, the pantry stocked, and all of the clutter we could sneak out of the house discarded. It was a daunting task, but we perservered.

Four weeks later we did it all over again. Multiply this by about four years, and you can see what we were up against. Looking back on it, I'm not sure how we managed to do it. We simply did what had to be done at the time.

Having both grown up in Roanoke, Marvin and I had a lot of good friends living there who opened up their homes and their hearts to us during this difficult time. We had friends who left their door keys under the mat for us if they were away, friends who let us stay in their home for Christmas, friends who laughed with us and cried with us, and fixed special meals for us when we were in town. We'll never forget their kindness.

I remember one meal in particular. We had spent a long snowy January day on the road from New York and arrived late at the home of our friend, Lois Way. We were tired and grumpy. As we limped through the front door, we were surprised to find a group of old friends inside waiting for us. It was an extraordinary moment.

A dinner party was about to start, and we were the guests of honor! We will never forget the warmth and camaraderie we shared around Lois's table on that cold January night. Neither will we forget her delicious meal.

She served a pasta, bean, and sausage casserole with Italian bread and a salad. It was elegant in its simplicity and was the perfect meal for hungry road warriors. I don't think Lois ever knew the impact her dinner had on us. I think sometimes it's the little things we remember in the midst of a crisis that we treasure the most. This is one of those things. Thanks, Lois!

Lois's White Bean and Sausage Rigatoni

8 ounces rigatoni pasta
8 ounces smoked sausage (I add more)
1/2 (10 oz.) package frozen chopped spinach, thawed
Two 14½ ounce cans stewed tomatoes
15 ounce can great northern beans, rinsed and drained
1/4 cup chicken broth
1 ½ teaspoons Italian seasoning
1/2 cup grated Parmesan cheese

Cook and drain pasta. Slice and fry smoked sausage. Mix everything except the Parmesan cheese in a 2-quart casserole. Sprinkle with cheese and bake uncovered at 375 degrees for 15-20 minutes, or until hot and bubbly.

Serves 6

Gina, Bailey, and Neil at Ocean City, Maryland – 2004
Gina's spaghetti sauce is simply the best I've ever eaten. Period.

Gina's Spaghetti Sauce

I've always thought of Italian food as comfort food—right up there on the list with meatloaf and mashed potatoes. Let's face it, spaghetti with meatballs, lasagna, and chicken parmesan are firmly entrenched in American cuisine. Almost every town has an Italian restaurant you can count on to be comfortable, casual, familiar, and with similar menu choices.

The typical Italian restaurant I remember from the 1950s and the 1960s had red and white checkered tablecloths and was dimly lit. Candles on each table were inserted into Chianti wine bottles. Dean Martin and Frank Sinatra crooned "Volare" and other Italian songs in the background. Waiters with aprons and fake Italian accents brought garlic bread to the table and took our order. We thought it was romantic.

In those days my mother, her friends, and my aunts all had what I swear was the same spaghetti sauce recipe. It was mostly canned tomato sauce, some garlic powder, and ground beef with a sprinkle of powdered Parmesan cheese on top, considered to be "foreign food".

Thankfully, we've come a long way since then. One thing that remains constant, however, is the love of a good spaghetti sauce. Almost everyone has a favorite spaghetti sauce recipe. I'm no exception.

The recipe I used for decades was robust and flavorful. I was perfectly happy with it until I visited my cousin Neil and his wife Gina.

She served spaghetti, and the sauce was fabulous. Hers was so much better than mine, that when I got home, I threw out my recipe and have been making Gina's ever since. It's simply the best spaghetti sauce I've ever eaten. Period.

Having said that, one day I got the bright idea to add another ingredient to it–fennel seed. I noticed that the Italian sausage had fennel seed in it so I figured "Why not add some more?" If I do say so myself, it was a stroke of genius. This subtle change gives a new depth of flavor to this already perfect sauce.

No one has ever been able to figure out what I added to Gina's spaghetti sauce until now. The secret is out. Can you say "fennel"?

Gina's Spaghetti Sauce

1 lb. meat (1/2 lb. ground Italian sausage and 1/2 lb. ground beef)
1 cup chopped onion
2 cloves garlic, minced
3 tablespoons olive oil
Two 16 ounce cans "no salt added" diced tomatoes, undrained
Two 6 ounce cans tomato paste
1 cup liquid (1/2 cup dry red wine and 1/2 cup water)
1 tablespoon sugar
1 1/2 teaspoons salt
1 1/2 teaspoons dried oregano
1/2 teaspoon pepper
1 tablespoon fennel seeds, crushed
1 bay leaf

In large heavy pan, cook meat, onion and garlic in oil until onion and garlic are tender crisp but not brown. Add remaining ingredients to the meat mixture. Simmer, uncovered, stirring occasionally, for 1 hour. Remove bay leaf.

Makes about 6 cups

VEGETABLES, CASSEROLES, AND SIDE DISHES

"What? We never smoked on the roof!"   *"Do you think they fell for it?"*
Marguerite (Slick) and Joy

Slick's Marinated Asparagus

I got my recipe for Marinated Asparagus from my good friend, Marguerite Alvis. She is a great cook and loves to entertain. She and I both learned these skills from our mothers, who were good friends. Even though neither Marguerite nor I had any idea what our mothers were doing in the kitchen, we learned somehow. Through osmosis, I guess.

Marguerite and I have known each other since we were in diapers. We used to occasionally get into trouble together as kids—nothing serious, however. Our parents used the word "mischievous" to describe us.

I spent the best summer of my life with the Alvises. Marguerite and I were sophomores in high school.

My parents were going to South America to travel and to attend the Baptist World Alliance in Rio de Janerio. I had the opportunity to go with them. Picture a sixteen- year-old making a decision like this. (A) I could go with my parents and a bunch of Baptist preachers to attend meetings and follow them around in foreign countries for weeks on end, or (B) I could stay with Marguerite, date boys, and cruise around town without my parents knowing. The boys and cars won.

Marguerite and I got away with a lot that summer and got grounded only twice. Mr. Alvis caught us coming home REALLY late from a date, and he also caught us smoking on the roof. We were busted on both counts.

There was a small roof outside of Marguerite's bedroom window. We would climb out there at night and smoke, throwing our cigarette butts as far as we could into the back yard. It never occurred to us that anyone would find them. Mr. Alvis did.

He made us clean up the backyard and promise to quit smoking. From then on, we didn't smoke—on the roof, that is. We waited until we were around the corner from the house before we lit up.

Marguerite and I are still friends. After she got married and had kids, she was nicknamed Slick. I'm not sure when she became Slick, but the name certainly suits her.

Slick's flair for decorating, cooking, and entertaining is well known. I have some of her party recipes, and they are extraordinary. The one I use the most is for marinated asparagus. The combination of canned asparagus, chopped red bell peppers, and minced onions in a sweet marinade is amazing. It's colorful, brimming with flavor, and perfect for a buffet dinner.

Slick and I stopped smoking after college. We know how to cook. Our mothers would be relieved.

Slick's Marinated Asparagus

3 cans asparagus spears, drained
1/2 cup vinegar
1/2 cup sugar
1/3 cup vegetable oil
1/2 cup red bell peppers, chopped fine
½ cup minced onion

Put vinegar and sugar in a small saucepan over low heat. Stir until sugar is dissolved. Add oil and heat until hot, not boiling. Add peppers and onions.

In a serving dish, place half of the asparagus spears in a single layer. Pour half of the hot mixture over it. Layer the rest of the asparagus on top, and cover with remaining mixture.

Cover, and refrigerate overnight, at least. This keeps well for several days.

Serves 6-8

Mrs. Tucker—1968
I was convinced that Mrs. Tucker must be one of the finest cooks in Virginia. I was right.

Mrs. Tucker's Scalloped Onions

My first job in the "real world" after college was teaching English at Nelson County High School in Lovingston, Virginia. It was 1966, and my husband was just starting his first year of graduate business school at the University of Virginia.

One of us had to pay the rent, so I took the job in Nelson County, a 30-minute drive from Charlottesville. I made all of $3,800 the first year and, after a big raise, $4,500 the following year.

I was about to teach Shakespeare, about which I knew nothing, to college bound seniors who were only four years younger than I. To say that I was absolutely terrified would be an understatement. Before my students arrived on the first day of school, I hid in my classroom closet and cried.

Somehow I bluffed my way through that day and the two years that followed. To my knowledge, no students were educationally harmed during this time. As far as I know, they went on to live perfectly normal lives.

I carpooled with four other teachers whose husbands also were in graduate school. We all were fresh out of college, newlyweds, inexperienced, and blissfully unaware of just how poor we really were.

The local teachers in Nelson County welcomed us with open arms, even though they knew we'd be leaving after a year or two when our husbands earned their degrees. They couldn't have been kinder and more helpful, which was a good thing because, Lord knows, I needed all the help I could get.

A fellow teacher named Mrs. Boyd Tucker invited us to lunch at her home on the last day of school. Mrs. Tucker was a refined soft-spoken woman, proud of her Southern heritage.

When we arrived at her house on that hot June day, we were astounded at the breathtaking array of chilled salads and desserts waiting for us. It was one of the best "going away parties" I'd ever attended. I left there convinced that Mrs. Tucker was one of the finest cooks in Virginia.

Well guess what—it turns out she was. Years later, I browsed through my first cookbook, "Recipes from Old Virginia", for inspiration. There, in the vegetable section, appeared a recipe for scalloped onions by Mrs. Boyd Tucker of Nelson County. Inclusion in this almost sacred book of Virginia recipes was a real coup. It was sort of a "Who's Who" of Virginia cooks at the time.

Naturally, I tried Mrs. Tucker's scalloped onions. They were simple, old-fashioned, and good—just like my mother would have made. The recipe says it's good with "pork chops and minute steak" but I think this great southern side dish would go with just about anything. I'd give this recipe an A+.

Mrs. Tucker's Scalloped Onions

6 large onions
4 tablespoons butter (or bacon fat)
Salt, pepper
2 slices white bread, crumbled
1 cup grated cheddar cheese
Paprika

Skin and slice onions. Melt butter in a skillet, and sauté onions until they are tender. Season with salt and pepper to taste. Place in a shallow baking dish.

Top with soft breadcrumbs, grated cheese, and sprinkle with paprika. Bake in 350-degree oven until crumbs are brown, about 15 minutes.

Serves 4

My beloved cheesy scalloped potatoes were gone, all gone, in a matter of minutes

Cheesy Scalloped Potatoes

Our children were lucky enough to go to a high school with a foreign exchange program. Sleepy Hollow High School in New York and the high school in Renningen, Germany, participated. The German kids came to Sleepy Hollow for three weeks in the fall, and our students went to Renningen in the spring. It was a win-win experience for everyone.

We volunteered as hosts for a German student each fall. In the first three years we hosted two delightful girls and one not so delightful boy. This boy was caught with beer on the football field, stayed out late, left a trail of dirty clothes and wet towels from his bedroom to the shower, and lost his passport the day before he was to leave. We will never forget him.

After our children had graduated and left home, we began welcoming the German teachers who accompanied the students to Sleepy Hollow. For the next three years we hosted two delightful teachers and one not so delightful teacher named Reiner.

Reiner was an oddball who lurked around the house and kept his bedroom door locked at all times. He roamed our neighborhood without telling us, so we never knew whether he was in or out of the house. He simply disappeared.

Actually we saw very little of him—except at dinnertime. Like clockwork he would magically appear in the kitchen when it was time to eat, even though I hadn't called anyone to the table yet. He would sit and wait to be served. If food was already on the table, he would start without us.

The night that he ate ALL of our favorite potato dish before we got to the table was the cruelest blow of all. My beloved cheesy scalloped potatoes were gone, all gone, in a matter of minutes. I couldn't believe it. These potatoes became our nightly dinner special for the remainder of his visit.

To this day, I still think of Reiner every time I make this dish. It remains one of our favorites. Even though my husband doesn't like cheese, he likes my cheesy scalloped potatoes. The combination of potatoes, green peppers, and pimentos in a light cheese sauce is as pretty to look at as it is to eat.

Keep in mind, it must be REALLY good if someone can eat an entire bowl of it in one sitting. Just in case, double the recipe.

Cheesy Scalloped Potatoes

4 cups diced potatoes
1 green pepper, chopped
4 ounce jar diced pimentos
Salt and pepper to taste

Slowly boil potatoes in water for 5 to 10 minutes—no more. Pour into a colander and drain. Put drained potatoes in a baking dish, and gently stir in chopped green peppers and pimentos. Add salt and pepper.

Cheese Sauce

2 tablespoons butter
2 tablespoons flour
1 teaspoon salt
½ teaspoon pepper
1 cup milk
1 cup grated cheddar cheese

In a medium saucepan melt butter. Add flour and stir with a whisk. Add salt and pepper and gradually add the milk, whisking constantly. Stir in grated cheese until the sauce is smooth.

Pour the cheese sauce evenly over the potatoes. Bake in a 400 degree oven for 30 minutes. Serve hot.

Serves Reiner, or 4 normal people.

The Summer of 1953
We rode our bikes everywhere, and if we were lucky, chased a speeding fire truck to its destination.

Ring Tum Diddy

Of all my childhood memories, the summer ones are the most vivid. Summer was a time to enjoy the simple things in life. I went barefoot, searched for four-leaf clovers in the yard, played on my swing, and carefully dissected honeysuckle flowers to taste the tiny drop of sweet nectar in each one. The nectar is tantalizingly good, by the way.

My grandmother taught me how to tie a long piece of thread to a June bug's leg and let it go. The June bug flew around as I held the thread, fascinated by my new toy. It was sort of a primitive remote control airplane, if you will. When I got tired of it, the thread was removed and the June bug was none the worse for the wear.

My friends and I rode our bikes everywhere, and if we were lucky, chased a speeding fire truck to its destination. We spied on people, then rang their doorbells and hid. On a good day we went to the local swimming pool with enough extra money to buy ice cream.

One of my favorite things to do was to climb the tree in my backyard in the late afternoon and listen, undetected, to the sounds of our neighborhood. I could hear the clatter of pots and pans in the kitchen as my mother prepared dinner, the sound of people coming home from work, and the laughter of children playing with one another in their backyards.

Then, just before six o'clock, mothers started calling them in for dinner. The Hardys across the street blew a whistle. Someone on the next street over rang a bell. My favorite was when Mrs. Irvin called her daughter, Francis. It was a two octave call going from low to high with the emphasis on the second syllable. Fran-CIS! Mother just leaned out the back door and told me to come in.

There was an unwritten rule that dinner had to be at six o'clock. Everybody had dinner then. I'm not sure why, but you'd better be there - or else.

A summertime dinner at our house always featured fresh vegetables from Daddy's garden. One meal that I liked in particular was called Ring Tum Diddy. It was a simple dish of sautéed vegetables and cheese served over toast. We usually had a small salad or some chilled cucumbers and fresh tomatoes with it.

This meal sounds too easy, but it's satisfying and good. I've learned over the years that some of the best dishes are the simple ones. This is a perfect example.

Keep your summertime simple. Go barefoot, catch a June bug or two, smell the honeysuckle, and fix yourself some Ring Tum Diddy for dinner. Just be sure you eat at six o'clock – or else.

Ring Tum Diddy*

1/4 pound bacon
1 large green pepper, chopped
3 onions, chopped
3 large tomatoes, peeled and chopped
3 ears corn, kernels scraped off
Salt and pepper
1/4 pound American cheese, grated
8 slices toast

Cook bacon and set aside. Drain half of the bacon fat from the skillet. Cook the pepper and onions in the remaining fat until soft. Add the tomatoes and corn and sauté for a few minutes. Season to taste with salt and pepper. Just before serving add the cheese. Serve hot on toast. Top with crumbled bacon.

*I have no idea why this recipe is called Ring Tum Diddy. It just is.

Serves 4

Whitney Smith – Age 2
What didn't wither and die was devoured by rabbits, beetles, and caterpillars.

Zucchini Boats

I tried vegetable gardening once. It was in Richmond, Virginia, in 1977. I got the bright idea that we should have a garden in our backyard that year. It was our first, and last, attempt at living off the land.

By the time we rented the rototiller, bought the peat moss, topsoil, and fertilizer and put a small fence around it to keep the dog out, we had a real investment in this project. As far as I can remember, we planted tomatoes, peppers, zucchini, string beans, and some cucumbers.

It was a record setting hot, dry, summer that year. What didn't wither and die was devoured by rabbits, beetles, and caterpillars. My husband still talks about the $40 tomato and the $30 string bean we harvested that year.

The zucchini did manage to thrive for a while, however, and yielded some green giants. The photo above is our two-year-old daughter holding a gigantic zucchini. It's positive proof that we actually grew something.

From this brief attempt at gardening, I know one thing for sure. It's hard to kill zucchini. I now limit my gardening to flowers, herbs, and a few pepper plants.

If you've ever had a successful backyard vegetable garden, you probably know about the perils of planting zucchini. Chances are, by August, you've been up to your ankles in squash, and by September, you will have served it every way you can think of and will have given it to friends, neighbors, and co-workers.

If you'd like to see zucchini disappear like magic at your dinner table, help is here. It's a great recipe, called "Zucchini Boats". We enjoyed this wonderful dish at a friend's home years ago. I asked for the recipe and wrote down the simple ingredients on the bottom of a shopping list. That yellowed piece of paper is the only recipe I have for it. There are few instructions, and no measurements. I've just been "winging it" all these years and it's always good. I'll do the best I can to put it in the form of a recipe for you. Here goes:

Zucchini Boats

3 medium zucchini
1 cup grated cheddar cheese
1/4 cup mayonnaise
1/3 cup Parmesan cheese
1/2 teaspoon fresh ground pepper
Paprika

Cut off the ends of the zucchini. Parboil whole zucchini for 10 minutes. Remove from the water, and cool. Cut in half lengthwise. Cut each half into 2-inch pieces. Scoop out pulp from the middle of each piece. Drain, cut side down, on paper towels. Blot excess moisture before filling.

Combine grated cheddar cheese and mayonnaise. Add Parmesan cheese and pepper, and mix well. Spoon cheese mixture into the zucchini "boats", and place them in a baking dish. Sprinkle tops with paprika.

Bake at 350 degrees for 25 minutes. Just before serving, put under the broiler to brown the tops. Serve immediately.

Note: These little "boats" are great for anything you like. Try filling them with cooked sausage topped with breadcrumbs, crabmeat mixed with a little mayonnaise and cheese, or stuff them like you would a taco, with ground beef, tomatoes, and onions. Use your imagination.

Makes 6 servings

Daddy (Jesse Davis – 1950)
"It wasn't a homegrown tomato that Eve ate, because she repented."

Homegrown Tomato Tart

I love tomatoes. I mean I really LOVE tomatoes—homegrown summer tomatoes, that is. There's nothing like them in the whole world. My father, a Baptist minister, used to joke that he knew for sure it wasn't a tomato that Eve ate, because she repented.

Daddy loved gardening. It was one of his great joys in life. He once told me that few things made him happier than working the soil with his hands.

As far as Daddy was concerned, the key to growing anything was cow manure. The more, the better. He referred to it as "black gold". We're not talking about the sanitized bags of manure we find today at garden centers. We're talking about REAL cow manure. He once loaded up the trunk of the car with buckets of the stuff at a farm in Richmond and drove the three hour trip home to Roanoke, smiling all the way.

I don't know if it was the T.L.C. or the manure that went into his garden, but we had the best vegetables I've ever eaten—especially the tomatoes. All summer and well into the fall, our kitchen windowsill was lined with tomatoes in various stages of ripeness. Some were oddly shaped and lopsided, and some were just huge. Daddy's tomatoes definitely were not perfect like the neatly packaged ones we find in the grocery store. The typical grocery store varieties are pretty, but tasteless. I'll choose the lumpy, homegrown kind every time.

During the summer months, when tomatoes are at their peak, feast on them while you can. One of my favorite ways to enjoy tomatoes is a tomato tart. It's an easy recipe that tastes as good as it looks. The key to making this wonderful dish is to drain your tomatoes well. If they're too juicy, the crust will be soggy. Other than that little tip, there's nothing complicated about making a tomato tart. Just assemble it, bake it, and eat it.

A tomato tart is a simple summer treat that's hard to beat. The secret ingredient? Lopsided homegrown tomatoes, of course.

Homegrown Tomato Tart

1 pie shell
Dijon mustard
1 cup grated cheese—Asiago, Romano, Gruyere, or Parmesan
Tomatoes, peeled and sliced *
Fresh herbs, chopped—Basil, thyme, oregano, rosemary, or sage
1 teaspoon minced garlic
2 tablespoons minced onion
2 tablespoons olive oil

Partially bake pie shell for 10 minutes at 425 degrees. Cool. Brush the bottom of the shell with Dijon mustard. Cover with freshly grated cheese. (A combination of Asiago and Romano is good, or use whatever you like.)

Drain tomatoes on paper towels until all liquid is absorbed. Layer tomatoes on top of cheese, filling pie shell. Sprinkle top with your favorite fresh herbs, garlic, and onions. Drizzle with olive oil. If the edge of the piecrust is browned, crimp some foil around it before baking to prevent it from burning.

Bake 20 minutes at 425 degrees. Let set for 5 minutes before slicing.

*I like to use a combination of red and yellow tomatoes, overlapping them for color contrast.

Serves 6

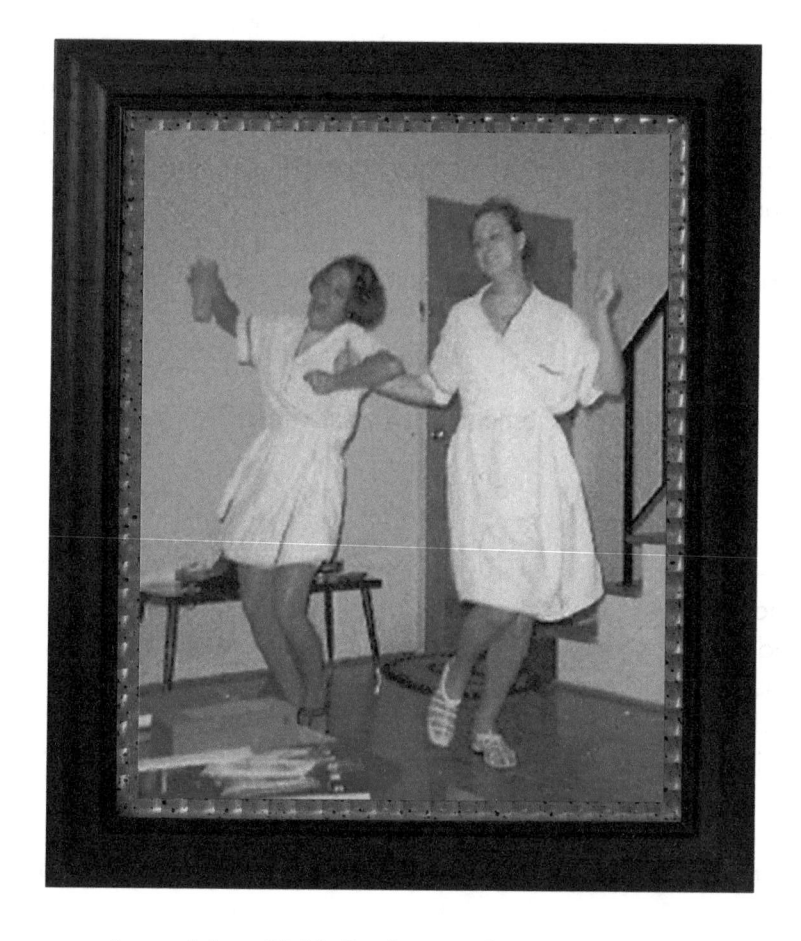

Joy and Anne Zirkle Performing the "Dance of Joy"
Even if you normally don't eat your potatoes first, you will after you taste this dish.

Anne's Mashed Potato Casserole

Have you ever noticed how many people eat the starchy food on their plate first? Well I have, because I'm one of them. Whether it's a potato dish, rice, or macaroni and cheese, I just can't help digging into it before anything else. It's a habit I have no intention of breaking.

I'm also one of those people who eats one thing at a time, but that's another story. Like other people I've met (yes, there are others), this is the way I like to eat. As a matter of fact, it took me well into adulthood before I could eat food that was touching other food on my plate. I really have come a long way, but I still like those picnic plates with dividers in them.

Back to the starchy foods. Even if you don't eat your potatoes first, you're going to be tempted to do so when you try the recipe I'm about to share with you. It's called Anne's Mashed Potato Casserole, and it's fabulous.

I've made this recipe for so long, I don't even bother to measure the ingredients anymore. I can't remember exactly when I started making it. My friend, Anne Zirkle, whose recipe it is, can't remember when she gave it to me. All I know for sure is that it's neatly typed on an index card, which dates it back to the early seventies.

I went through a very short-lived phase of typing recipes when I first started cooking. I wanted them to look pretty and to fit perfectly into my new little recipe box. About 10 recipes into this project, I realized the folly of it and started jotting them down on scratch paper, napkins, check stubs, or whatever was handy at the time.

Mashed Potato Casserole is one of our favorite side dishes. It's simple, delicious, and can be made ahead of time. You can even make potato pancakes with the leftovers.

I love to serve these potatoes when we have company. It's a perfect side dish for almost any entrée, and everybody likes them. Dinner guests inevitably say, "I love these potatoes," followed by, "Could I please have the recipe?"

If you want to wow your guests with a simple potato dish, try this one. Keep some recipe cards handy to give out at the end of the night. You're going to need them.

Anne's Mashed Potato Casserole *

One 8 ounce package softened cream cheese
4 cups hot mashed potatoes
1 egg, beaten
1/3 cup finely chopped onion
1/2 cup chopped pimento
1 teaspoon salt
Dash of pepper

Combine softened cream cheese and potatoes until well blended. Stir in the other ingredients. Place in casserole and bake, uncovered, at 350 degrees for 45 minutes.

Serves 4

*Potato pancakes can be made with the leftovers. Refrigerate leftover casserole. When ready to serve, shape potatoes into patties. Sauté in a little olive oil until browned on each side. These are a great substitute for hash browns or home fried potatoes.

"Hey look! I'm not a grit snob anymore!"

The Dreaded Grit Casserole

In 1968, my husband Marvin and I moved to Charlotte, North Carolina, from Charlottesville, Virginia. He had just completed graduate business school at the University of Virginia and had accepted a job with Burlington Industries.

I needed a job too, and against all odds was offered a position as a fifth grade teacher in Belmont, North Carolina, despite the fact that I knew nothing about elementary education. Obviously, they were desperate.

Teaching fifth grade was a HUGE learning experience for me. I had about twenty-five kids in my class, and I was responsible for teaching them everything. I mean everything. English, math, science, art, physical education, music, etc. You name it, I taught it.

I was with my students all day, including lunch. The cafeteria food left a lot to be desired. No matter what the entrée was, we seemed to have some sort of grits on our plates every day. There were buttered grits, cheese grits, grit cakes, grit casseroles, and just plain grits. Having never been exposed to this southern specialty before, eating grits was a new experience for me.

The kids seemed to like them, but I soon discovered that I really hated grits with a passion. I added them to my list of disgusting foods that I never intended to eat again, which included liver, collard greens, and Brussels sprouts.

Marvin and I moved to Greensboro the following year. From Greensboro, Marvin's career took us to Richmond, Virginia, Sleepy Hollow, New York, and, much to our delight, back to the Charlotte area in 1998. Thirty years later we were right back where we started and right back to where the dreaded grits were served wherever we went.

I refused to eat any dish that had the word grit in it, which turned out to be really stupid. I was a grit snob.

Years passed, and not a single grit crossed my lips. And then it happened. I attended a lovely brunch at the home of a friend and tried her special cheesy casserole with tomatoes in it. It was creamy and delicious. I went back for seconds. And thirds.

Naturally I asked for the recipe and was aghast when I found out that it was a grit casserole. I took the recipe anyway and have been happily enjoying it since. It's been a long road from the Belmont elementary school's daily dose of grits to this fabulous casserole but it was worth the journey. I am a grit snob no more.

The Dreaded Grit Casserole

1 ¼ cups milk
2 cups water
1 teaspoon salt
1 cup quick cooking grits
1 stick (1/2 cup) butter, plus 1 tablespoon butter
1/2 cup diced scallions
4 ounce Velveeta cheese, cubed
2 ½ cups shredded extra sharp cheddar cheese
10 ounce can Rotel tomatoes

In a large saucepan, bring milk and water to a boil. Add the salt and slowly stir in the grits. Return to a boil, stirring constantly for 1 minute. Reduce the heat, cover, and cook for 3 minutes. Stir in ½ cup of butter and continue stirring until the butter is melted. Cover and cook for 4 minutes, or until the grits are thick and creamy. Remove from heat and set aside.

Saute diced scallions in the remaining tablespoon of butter for 1 minute. Add the cheeses and sautéed scallions to the grits and stir until the cheese is melted. Add the tomatoes and mix well. Pour the grits into a greased 8 x 11 x 2 inch casserole and bake for 40 minutes at 350 degrees. Serve hot.

Serves 8-10

Joy (age 4) and friends enjoying a ride at the church picnic.
After an unbearably long blessing, we dove into the mounds of food with reckless abandon.

Church Picnic Bean Casserole

Without a doubt, our church picnic was one of the highlights of the summer when I was a kid. Virginia Heights Baptist Church in Roanoke, threw one whale of a picnic every year. This wasn't your average church picnic, either. After all, it was held at Lakeside, a gem of an amusement park in town.

As with any amusement park, there were cotton candy and snow cones to eat, a fun house to scare everyone, and rides guaranteed to thrill even the most seasoned amusement park veteran.

My favorite ride was the roller coaster. This fabulous old-fashioned wooden roller coaster's first very steep hill never failed to take my breath away. I get butterflies in my stomach just thinking about it.

We always enjoyed a great turnout for the church picnic. We occupied the biggest picnic shelter on the grounds. Each child ran off to use their fistful of free tickets, returning a couple hours later deliriously happy, somewhat disheveled, and famished.

The men of the church cooked hot dogs and hamburgers for us, while the church ladies unveiled their homemade picnic fare. A splendid display of potato salads, baked beans, pies, and cakes, were laid out on the long tables. The feast could have fed the proverbial 5,000.

After what seemed to be an unbearably long blessing, we dove into the mounds of food with reckless abandon. I went straight for my mother's baked beans. Some of the bean dishes had strips of bacon across the top for extra flavor, but Mother's had flavor baked right into them. She added molasses, catsup, brown sugar, and mustard to her beans before cooking them. They were terrific.

I still make Mother's recipe, but I substitute barbecue sauce for the catsup and add a dash of liquid smoke. I don't think she'd mind these subtle changes.

I came across a recipe several years ago that I like more than Mother's beans, believe it or not. It's perfect for picnics and parties, big or small.

Going to a picnic this summer? Wow the crowds with this delicious bean dish. I'm sure the church ladies would have loved it.

Church Picnic Bean Casserole

4 slices bacon
1 large onion, sliced
16 ounce can lima beans, drained
16 ounce can pork and beans in tomato sauce
15 1/2 ounce can red kidney beans, drained
7 1/2 ounce can diced tomatoes
1/4 cup packed brown sugar
1 tablespoon Worcestershire sauce
1/2 teaspoon dry mustard

In a medium skillet, cook bacon until crisp. Drain bacon on paper towels. Pour all but 2 tablespoons of bacon drippings from skillet. Cook onions in reserved drippings until tender, but not brown.

In a 2-quart casserole, combine crumbled bacon, onion, lima beans, undrained pork and beans, kidney beans, and undrained tomatoes. Stir in brown sugar, Worcestershire sauce, and dry mustard.

Bake, covered, in a 375-degree oven for 40 minutes. Uncover and bake for 25 minutes more.

Serves 10.

I warmed up to the idea of getting older as soon as the monetary factor kicked in.

Lori's Pineapple Casserole

I've learned a lot about life since I crossed that line between 64 and 65 years old. At 64, I was a nobody but at 65, I suddenly become "mature". In some circles I'm referred to as an "active adult". I get "wisdom" discounts at the grocery store, free "senior" drinks at some fast food chains, a "Silver Sneakers" class to join at the gym, and an invitation to open a "Springtimers Club" account at my credit union.

I've learned that I can get all sorts of things for less money. I can go to the movies cheaper, order from a special section of the menu in some restaurants, and get discounts on everything from county fairs to hotel rooms. I warmed up to the idea of being older really quickly once the monetary factor kicked in.

Other lessons learned weren't so great. My mail changed. Suddenly I was bombarded with advertisements for hearing aids and life insurance policies.

One of the most annoying things that happened was that people began calling me "young lady". I haven't been called "young lady" since I was a teenager coming home after my curfew, and my father used a much different tone of voice.

One of the funniest things that happened was that I was asked for my ID at a museum in order to get the senior discount. I haven't been carded since I was buying beer at age 21. I loved it.

One of the most important things I've learned is how to say two little words - "no" and "yes". I used to worry what people would think if I turned down a request to chair a committee, host a luncheon, or be an officer of an organization. Not any more. I discovered that there are plenty of other people to do these jobs and that I wasn't as important as I thought I was.

Saying "yes" is sometimes as difficult as saying "no". I worried that people would think I wasn't capable of running an event by myself if I had to ask for help. This is a matter of pride.

I got over that pride in a hurry the year I needed help with our annual Christmas party. I was recovering from surgery and there was no way I could prepare all the food myself. I said yes to friends who wanted to bring additions to the buffet. That was a brilliant decision. The food was awesome.

One of the best dishes came from my next-door neighbor, Lori Bowers. Her pineapple casserole was to die for. Everybody loved it. I've been serving it every year since then and have given her recipe to countless people. Now I'm giving it to you.

Here's my advice to go with this recipe. If you're old enough to get the wisdom discount at the grocery store, you're old enough to have learned this lesson. Just say yes to offered food. Good things happen.

Lori's Pineapple Casserole

2 large cans chunk pineapple
2/3 cup sugar
5 teaspoons flour
1 ½ cups grated extra sharp cheddar cheese
1 sleeve buttery crackers, crushed (I use Ritz crackers)
1 stick melted butter

Mix together pineapple, sugar, flour, and cheese. Put in casserole dish. In a separate bowl, pour melted butter over cracker crumbs and mix well. Spread on top of pineapple mixture.

Cook in a 350-degree oven for 30-40 minutes.

Serves 6-8

Joy and Leo – 1951
I printed Leo's name on an ornament in my best first grader's handwriting and put glitter on it.

Tipsy Pineapple

Christmas is absolutely my favorite time of the year. With a name like Joy, I feel like a real celebrity. After all, in December my name is everywhere. It's in stores, catalogs, and church bulletins. It's on billboards, Christmas cards, magazine covers, and ornaments. You name it, Joy has probably been there. Even as a little girl I knew that Christmas was all about "Joy".

One of the things I most enjoy is unpacking my Christmas decorations. It's like being reunited with old friends every year. Each piece represents a special memory of my childhood, of loved ones, places we've lived, trips we've taken, those dear ones handmade by the children, LOTS of "Joy" ornaments, and even the pets we've had.

I've made an ornament for every pet I've ever had. The oldest one was for my big, yellow cat Leo in 1951. I painted his name on it in my very best first grader's handwriting, dated it, and sprinkled glitter on it. Tragically, it fell off the tree in 2011 and broke. I still haven't gotten over it. It was the first time in 60 years that Leo wasn't represented on the family Christmas tree. He might be gone, but certainly is not forgotten.

Once decorated, our home and our tree tell the story of our family's history. This includes things my mother collected over the years: the big pinecone wreath she made, the manger that Daddy and I built out of an orange crate, and ornaments that belonged to my grandmother.

Aside from the nostalgic joys of decorating, you might guess that I love to cook and entertain at this time of the year. You'd be right.

Throwing a good Christmas party has been a Smith tradition for years. I make notes after the party is over noting what was devoured and what was left over. I make some revisions, but the majority of the menu stays the same. The party just wouldn't be the same without ham biscuits, pork tenderloin, my Aunt Esther's Swedish meatballs, smoked salmon, several salads, chilled marinated asparagus, deviled eggs, and shrimp aspic.

At the suggestion of my friend, Jerrie Frye, I added a dish called Tipsy Pineapple. The Frye's have a Christmas party at their home every year, and this treat is always popular. According to Jerrie, one guest in particular positions himself strategically next to the pineapple so he can have unlimited access to it. This testimony was so compelling that I decided to serve it. The results were predictable. It was a big hit.

This dish is extremely easy to make, and can be made well in advance. As a matter of fact, the longer it sits, the better it gets. It's a perfect addition to any buffet table and a delicious side dish to compliment almost any entree. You're going to love it. So will your guests.

Tipsy Pineapple

1 pineapple, cored
1 cup sugar
1/3 cup water
1/4 cup Triple Sec
1/4 cup fresh lime juice
Grated zest of 1 orange

Cut the pineapple into bite sized pieces. Put pieces into a bowl.

Combine sugar and water in a small saucepan and bring to a boil, stirring to dissolve the sugar. Remove from the heat and add the Triple Sec, lime juice, and orange zest. Mix well. Pour over the pineapple chunks. Cover and put into the refrigerator. Let marinate for at least a day, stirring several times.

Drain and serve.

Serves approximately 8-10

The Davis - Smith Nuptials, September 3, 1966
It only took them 30 years to get to know each other

Bouillon Rice

I can't remember whether I got this recipe for bouillon rice from my friend, Peggy Swink, or whether she got it from me. I guess it really doesn't matter. We both served it A LOT in the 1970s. Our husbands knew exactly what to expect for dinner when we got together. No matter what the entrée was, bouillon rice was sitting there next to it.

I absolutely love rice—always have, as a matter of fact. I have many rice recipes now, but bouillon rice was my very first. Because I love rice so much, I just assumed that my husband Marvin did too.

One night after about 30 years of marriage, I served rice for dinner. Something just snapped, and he blurted out, "I hate rice!" I asked, "Well, why didn't you say so sooner?" Good question.

On the other hand, it took him 30-some years to figure out that I couldn't read a road map. This became painfully obvious when we flew to California and landed in San Diego. Marvin drove the rental car while I reluctantly manned the map, turning it constantly to figure out which way was up. In no time, I had us headed directly for the Mexican border. In frustration I threw down the map and exclaimed, "I can't read a road map!" He asked, "Well, why didn't you say so sooner?" Good question.

Lessons learned. I no longer serve Marvin rice, and he reads the maps while I do the driving. I've decided that one of the keys to a good marriage is getting to know each other really well. Obviously, for some of us it takes longer than others.

Even though Marvin isn't a fan of bouillon rice, I can heartily recommend it. Serve this wonderful rice dish at your next dinner party. You and your guests will love it. Just don't invite Marvin.

Bouillon Rice

½ stick butter
1 small onion, minced
1 cup rice
1 cup beef bouillon
1 cup consommé
One 7 ounce can sliced mushrooms, drained

Brown minced onion in butter. Combine rice, bouillon, and consommé together in a baking dish. Stir in the browned onions and add the mushrooms. Cover.

Bake at 350 degrees for 30 minutes. Remove cover and bake for another 30 minutes. Serve hot.

Serves 4-6

SALADS AND SALAD DRESSINGS

Non-salad eaters can graze their way through this and eventually find something they like.

Sensational Sesame Spinach Salad

When the weather's hot, my thoughts turn to light foods and salads – especially salads. Without a doubt I consume more leafy greens from May to September than in all the other months combined.

If I had to pick just one salad as my favorite, I'd have to choose one called Sensational Sesame Spinach Salad (try saying this 5 times fast – I double dog dare you). This is the one I serve over and over again. I figure when something is this good, stick with it.

The dressing for this salad is what sets it apart from all the others. It's a deeply flavored toasted sesame dressing that's addictive. The best part is that you can make it in the blender and keep it in the refrigerator until you're ready to use it.

I use the word spinach loosely in the name of this salad. I've used all sorts of lettuce to make it. I also throw in extra ingredients I have on hand at the time. The only things that remain constant are tomatoes, oranges, red onions, mushrooms, dressing (of course), and honey roasted cashews sprinkled over the top. Cashews are quite simply the crowning touch (or the "cat's meow" as I like to say) to this wonderful salad.

When making this dish for a crowd, be sure to make plenty of it. Sometimes I even use a big punch bowl so I'll have enough. I've found that even those who normally don't like salad can graze their way through this one and eventually find something they like.

If it's summer, eat salad. This salad.

Sensational Sesame Spinach Salad*

1½ pounds spinach (substitute a mix of different lettuces if you like)
11 ounce can mandarin orange slices, drained
½ cup red onion, thinly sliced
1 pint cherry tomatoes, halved
8 ounce package sliced mushrooms
1 cup seedless red or green grapes
Honey roasted cashews to taste

To assemble the salad, put all the ingredients in a large bowl. Mix well so ingredients are evenly distributed. When ready to serve, pour the following sesame dressing over it, tossing lightly to coat the spinach. Scatter those sweet, crunchy, nutty cashews on top and serve.

*Measurements are approximate. Make it any way you want. I like to add sliced radishes, strips of red and yellow bell peppers, and dried cranberries for extra color, flavor, and crunch. It's a great way to stretch this salad to feed a big group.

Serves 4-6

Sesame Dressing*

6 tablespoons vegetable oil
2 tablespoons cider vinegar
2 tablespoons honey
2 tablespoons Dijon mustard
2 tablespoons toasted sesame seeds
1 clove garlic, minced
½ teaspoon pepper

Put all ingredients in a blender. Blend on low until smooth, scraping down the sides with a spatula as needed. Pour into container and store in refrigerator until needed.

*Double or triple this recipe depending on the size of your salad. Keep the leftover dressing in the refrigerator. Supposedly this dressing keeps for quite a while, but I wouldn't know. There's never any left over at our house.

Makes 1 cup

Not a good sign

Tuna Salad

In a perfect world dining out would be a joy. Restaurants would be filled with an attentive wait staff, polite patrons, and perfectly cooked food served in a timely manner. The ambience would create a place where you could retreat from a hectic life to an oasis of quiet relaxation.

Unfortunately, it's not a perfect world. I know this for sure. My husband and I have experienced almost every restaurant scenario you can imagine. We've been seated next to families with unruly children and crying babies, people shouting into their cell phones, couples arguing with each other, and large groups of loud women. (Sorry ladies, but you ARE louder than men – sports bars excluded.)

We've had waiters who ignored us, forgot to turn in our order, dropped our food coming out of the kitchen, brought us someone else's meal, and unfortunately, sang to us. Marvin even had a waitress quit in the middle of serving him and some business associates. She took their order and left – permanently.

We've witnessed break-ups, make-ups, seduction, and near death experiences while dining. The near death experience was a fellow diner choking on a piece of steak. Thankfully he was resuscitated by a quick thinking patron who performed the Heimlich maneuver on him. Now that's a meal to remember!

My father had two rules when it came to restaurants. (1) Go where there are lots of cars in the parking lot. (2) Avoid places with an "Under New Management" sign in the window. This turns out to be pretty good advice.

We've discovered that sometimes you can go to a favorite restaurant one too many times. You can find that it has changed, and not for the better. Unfortunately, this does happen.

A perfect example of this is a sandwich shop that Marvin frequented for lunch every Friday for about 10 years. Just like clockwork he showed up for the Friday special, a tuna salad sub sandwich. The staff automatically made him his sandwich just the way he liked it – tuna, no mayonnaise, with lettuce and pepper – when he walked through the door.

Then one Friday he arrived to find lots of dirty tables and a new staff who couldn't care less that he was there. The "Under New Management" rule struck a fatal blow to Marvin's favorite lunchtime haunt.

Being suddenly without his favorite tuna salad, he came home and asked if I knew how to make it. "Everybody should have a good tuna salad recipe," he said. Well I didn't.

After several failed attempts, I finally found a recipe that passed Marvin's stringent test of what tuna salad should taste like. Because he thinks everyone should know how to make good tuna salad, I'm passing this recipe along to you. Try it on a sub roll with lettuce and pepper and see what you think. It works for Marvin.

Tuna Salad

Two (6 ounce) cans tuna in water (or packages of tuna in water)
2 tablespoons freshly squeezed lemon juice
1 teaspoon salt
½ teaspoon pepper
1 stalk of celery, minced
2 tablespoons red onion, minced
2 tablespoons pickle relish
2 tablespoons minced fresh Italian parsley
½ cup mayonnaise
1 teaspoon Dijon mustard

Drain the tuna well. Put it in a bowl and add the lemon juice, salt, pepper, celery, red onion, relish, and parsley. Gently mix them together. Fold in the mayonnaise and mustard until the tuna mixture is evenly coated.

Serve it on your favorite bread with a nice deli pickle on the side.

Makes 2 cups

Mommie (Sarah McDuell Lavisson—1954)
The culprit in the "Great Tulip Bulb Caper"

Mommie's Mashed Potato Salad

Lots of families have some sort of a recipe that has spanned the generations. In my case, the recipe is from my mother's family, the Lavissons. Their mashed potato salad is a chilled, tart version of potato salad. It was my grandmother's recipe, passed on to her five daughters, and now on to my cousins and me.

My grandmother, Sarah McDuell Lavisson, was known as "Sadie" to her friends and family, and "Mommie" to us grandchildren. She was a large woman with a great sense of humor and an ample lap for holding children. I remember that lap being a warm, happy place to be.

Mommie lived with my Aunt Flora, Uncle Harry, and my cousin Bonnie on a beautiful farm in Ednor, Maryland. Mother's other sisters all lived reasonably close by, so our summer visits there were real family affairs.

With all of my aunts, uncles, and cousins around, there was never a dull moment with the Lavission family. At the center of these get-togethers was Mommie.

Mommie was an excellent seamstress and was always busy with needlework of some sort, usually crocheting. I still have some of her handiwork—a little crocheted bear and some beautifully detailed clothes she made for my dolls.

This talented woman also made lovely flower-shaped beaded pins, each uniquely crafted with small colorful beads on delicate wire. I distinctly remember my mother wearing those pins on her coats and dresses.

Years ago, I came across several of Mommie's beaded pins tucked away in a small box of my mother's belongings. When I opened that box, I felt as if I had won the lottery. I was thrilled.

As for Mommie's cooking skills, I'll never forget her role in what we called the "Great Tulip Bulb Caper". Helping out with dinner one evening, she inadvertently cut up Aunt Flora's tulip bulbs instead of the onions sitting next to them on the counter. Fortunately, they realized the mistake before it became part of dinner. To this day I can't look at a tulip bulb without wondering what it would taste like in meatloaf.

Because it's served chilled, mashed potato salad is a great recipe for summertime dinners and picnics. It's not your average potato salad, believe me. With Mommie in mind, I'm happy to share this Lavission family specialty with you. Just make sure there aren't any tulip bulbs in it.

Mommie's Mashed Potato Salad*

8 medium potatoes, boiled and mashed
4 hard boiled egg yolks, mashed with 1 teaspoon dry mustard
1 cup vinegar
1/2 stick butter
1/2 cup chopped onion
3/4 cup chopped celery
Salt and pepper to taste

Heat vinegar and stir in butter and mashed egg yolks. Combine mashed potatoes with onion, celery, salt, and pepper. Add vinegar mixture and beat well. Chill.

*My mother added pickle relish to the salad, which apparently was a sacrilege. My Aunt Rena told me in no uncertain terms that there was absolutely no relish in it. The message was clear—don't mess with the recipe!

Serves 6-8

I love Willis Carrier, the genius who invented the air conditioner. God bless him.

French Potato Salad

Memorial Day Weekend is memorable at our house every year. Yes, it defines the beginning of summer, but it also marks the beginning of my summer hibernation. I go inside and don't come out (unless I have to) until Labor Day.

I really don't deal well with the heat—I never have and probably never will.

Thank God for air-conditioning. I grew up without it, so maybe that's why I'm so grateful for it now. I admit to keeping the house pretty cool in the summer. Years ago my husband came home from work and claimed that walking into our house was like stepping into a Siberian winter. A slight exaggeration—maybe.

We're definitely a "temperature challenged" couple. He's cold natured. I'm hot natured. Despite the ongoing battle for control of the thermostat, we've somehow managed to co-exist under the same roof since 1966.

When the temperature rises outside, I pull out my cookbooks and recipes in search of chilled soups, light entrees, fresh vegetable dishes, and salads. Salads win the prize for the most popular summer food, as far as I'm concerned. After all, there's an endless variety of ingredients that you can put together and still call it salad. Whether it's made from meat, fruit, seafood, pasta, rice, poultry, or vegetables, it can be a salad.

A perennial summer favorite is potato salad. It goes with practically everything, and is the cornerstone of any picnic. I love potato salad but find that the typical mayonnaise-based ones are a little heavy and sometimes bland.

I have a great recipe for potato salad that's a delightful change from the ordinary. It's called French Potato Salad. It's a simple salad of marinated and chilled cooked potato slices sprinkled with scallions and fresh parsley.

Enjoy this chilled salad on a hot day. Maybe you won't even need to turn on the air conditioner. Yeah, right!

French Potato Salad

6 large boiling potatoes
1/2 cup olive oil
1/4 cup tarragon vinegar
1/3 cup beef consommé
1 teaspoon salt
1/2 teaspoon freshly ground pepper
1 teaspoon Dijon mustard
Bibb lettuce
1/2 cup thinly sliced green onion
1/4 cup chopped parsley

Boil potatoes for 20 minutes, or until just tender. Cool slightly. Peel and slice into 1/4 inch slices. Combine oil, vinegar, consommé, salt, pepper, and mustard. Toss gently with sliced potatoes. Cover, and chill several hours or overnight. (Stir occasionally to evenly distribute marinade over potatoes.)

Spread leaves of Bibb lettuce on a serving plate. Spoon potato slices on the lettuce and sprinkle with green onions and parsley.

Serves 4-6

Welcome to Virginia Heights Baptist Church
Enjoy a recipe straight from the front row of my father's church. It's heavenly.

Kitchen Drawer Jell-O Salads

My mother was a packrat when it came to collecting recipes. There was a drawer in our kitchen full of miscellaneous stuff, including an incredible stash of recipes. She had recipes from every source imaginable – calendars, instruction sheets that came with appliances, pamphlets from local businesses, little cookbooks from her Sunday school class and her sorority, etc. Basically, anything that had a recipe on it went into that drawer.

Mother's kitchen drawer told a lot about her. She had a family with eclectic tastes, she loved to entertain, she had lots of friends, and she went to church a lot.

She went to church a lot because my father was a minister. Even if you didn't know this you'd still be able to guess this from her recipe collection. Some of Mother's recipes are written on pew cards – you know, those little cards on the pews for newcomers to fill in their information for the visitation committee? Well, apparently my mother had another use for them. In addition to recipes, I found some of these cards with grocery lists and doodles on them. She sat on the front pew every Sunday. Now I know what she was doing up there – at least part of the time.

I couldn't help but notice that a common thread runs through Mother's collection – Jell-O. Her entire generation was enamored with it. Apparently Jell-O was considered to be fine food back then. Featured in desserts, its main role was in salads.

The word Jell-O is replaced by the word "congealed" in most of the salad recipes. Maybe this was to make them sound more sophisticated or something. Frankly I think the word "congealed" is a little creepy and certainly unappetizing, but that's just my opinion.

Reading through the myriad of salad recipes I can't help but notice that the ingredients are pretty much the same—fruit, nuts, marshmallows, and Jell-O. The only difference seems to be what color they are, depending on what flavor of Jell-O is used.

As I thumbed through the multicolored salad recipes, my eyes began to glaze over. An orange one caught my attention, however. It was a molded salad featuring orange sherbet. It had only three ingredients – orange sherbet, orange Jell-O, and orange slices. No nuts or marshmallows to be found anywhere. I made it and it was great.

The thing that sets this recipe apart from the others and makes it particularly special to me is that it's written on the back of a church pew card in my mother's handwriting. Enjoy this recipe straight from the front row of my father's church. It's heavenly.

Mandarin Orange Salad

Two (3 ounce) packages of orange Jell-O
2 cups boiling water
1 pint orange sherbet
2 small cans mandarin oranges, drained

Dissolve Jell-O in boiling water. Cool. Stir in orange sherbet and mandarin orange slices. Pour into a greased mold and chill in the refrigerator until it's firm. Unmold onto a pretty dish and garnish with additional mandarin orange slices.

Serves 6

Raspberry Aspic*

Another congealed salad recipe from Mother's kitchen drawer intrigued me–a red one this time. This wasn't a salad recipe, however. It was an aspic. It, too, was void of any fruits, nuts and marshmallows, and it had only three ingredients in it–raspberry Jell-O, tomato juice, and horseradish. This intriguing combination of ingredients was irresistible.

I made it and found it to be different from any other aspic I've ever tasted–in a good way, that is. This is aspic with a kick. It has attitude. You bite it and it bites you back, depending on how much horseradish you put into it. Make it mild or spicy. Suit yourself.

3 ounce package of raspberry Jell-O
2 cups tomato juice (I use V8 juice)
1 tablespoon horseradish

Heat tomato juice to boiling point and add powdered Jell-O. Stir until Jell-O is dissolved. Add 1 tablespoon prepared horseradish and stir until well mixed. Pour into 1 large greased mold or small individual ones. Chill in refrigerator until set. Unmold and serve.

*Garnish with nuts and marshmallows. Just kidding!!!

Serves 4

Something fishy is going on here.

Shrimp Aspic

Among my favorite possessions are my cookbooks. They are reminders of places I've been, people I've met, special occasions, and dear friends. We're talking about cookbooks of all descriptions here—old, new, big, little, foreign, domestic, regional, silly, and serious. I have one for every occasion.

My oldest book is "The White House Cookbook" from 1912. It's actually falling apart, but I don't care. It's one of my favorites. Some of the VERY dated recipes are for squirrel stew, broiled pigeons, baked calf's head, and pickled pigs' feet. It's entertaining reading to say the least.

For years, I brought back a cookbook and a Christmas tree ornament from our travels as souvenirs. After filling up 3 bookcases with cookbooks, and having so many "Joy" ornaments that we had to add a second Christmas tree to hold them, I switched to refrigerator magnets and food. Of the souvenirs I've collected, the cookbooks are my favorite.

I read cookbooks the way most people read novels, except I take notes. As I read through them I make a list of the recipes that sound good, including the page number, and tuck the list inside the front cover for future reference. It saves lots of time later on when I'm looking for a particular recipe. It's the method that works for me – a real timesaver for sure.

I remember quickly thumbing through my lists looking for a nice chilled salad recipe to take to a luncheon one hot summer day. It didn't take long to find the perfect recipe, and it wasn't a salad that

I chose. It was an aspic—a shrimp aspic to be exact. As the weather gets warmer, a nice chilled aspic is a good substitute for a salad and can be served in individual molds or one large one.

Shrimp Aspic has been a favorite dish in our house for years. I like to spice it up with extra horseradish and hot sauce, but of course that's optional. You can easily double this recipe for a large group and make it days in advance if you like. Be sure to coat the inside of your molds with cooking spray before filling them so the aspic will slide out easily when it's firm.

Every time I've served this dish, it's been a hit. Served on a bed of lettuce leaves, surrounded with lemon wedges and extra pieces of shrimp, it's a stunning addition to the table. The next time you need a summer salad, think aspic. Shrimp aspic, that is.

Shrimp Aspic

3 ounce package lemon gelatin
1 cup boiling water
1/2 cup chili sauce
2 teaspoons horseradish
2 tablespoons vinegar
3 or 4 drops Tabasco
Water
1/2 pound cooked shrimp, cut in bite-size pieces

Mix gelatin with boiling water. Combine next 5 ingredients to measure a total of 1 cup. Add to gelatin and refrigerate until it begins to congeal. Add shrimp to the mixture and spoon into a greased 1 quart mold or into individual molds. Chill until firm.

Serves 6

Naked salads are waiting to get dressed. Don't peek.

Joy's Favorite Salad Dressings

I was a "Johnny Come Lately" (as my grandmother would say) to the homemade salad dressing world. The closest I came to making my own dressing was to whip up a batch of prepackaged ingredients with some oil, vinegar, and water in a cruet that came with it. I felt creative doing this.

It wasn't until I went to a friend's dinner party that I saw actual salad dressing being made from scratch. The hostess stepped into the kitchen and nonchalantly whisked some red wine vinegar, olive oil, salt and pepper together. She tossed a nice green salad with it, added some grated cheese and croutons and brought it to the table.

I was struck by the ease of preparing this simple salad and how good it tasted. Easy and good. Now that's my kind of recipe.

From that moment on I've become a salad dressing nut. There are as many variations as there are ingredients. I've learned that if something doesn't taste the way you like it, just keep adding ingredients until it does. If it's too tart, add some honey. If it's too sweet, add something acidic—like vinegar or citrus juice. Not enough flavor? Salt and pepper is your answer.

If you still hate what you've made, I have two words for you—prepackaged dressings. Mix it, shake it, and serve it in a glass cruet.

If you've never made your own dressing, now's your chance. I'm going to share a few of my favorites, so get a whisk and a bowl and let's get started. Your naked salad is waiting to get dressed.

Citrus Vinaigrette

½ cup extra virgin olive oil
¼ cup freshly squeezed lemon juice*
3 tablespoons white wine vinegar
3 tablespoons honey
Salt, pepper

Blend ingredients until combined. Taste for flavor. Add more lemon juice, honey, salt or pepper until it's perfect for you.

*Use lime juice or orange juice for a deliciously different citrus vinaigrette.

Note: If you are making orange vinaigrette, substitute orange marmalade for the honey and substitute orange vinegar for the white wine vinegar. Top the salad with mandarin orange slices for extra flavor.

Makes 1 cup

Sesame Soy Dressing

½ cup sesame oil
¼ cup soy sauce
¼ cup rice vinegar
1 teaspoon Dijon mustard
1 teaspoon honey
Salt, pepper

Put the first 5 ingredients in a blender. Blend until well mixed. Add salt and pepper to taste. Chill. It's particularly good with a chopped salad of romaine lettuce, red cabbage, and shredded carrots. Top with crunchy soy nuts or peanuts.

Makes 1 cup

Miso Dressing

2 tablespoons miso
4 tablespoons honey
Juice of 2 lemons

Whisk the ingredients together and chill. Serve over a simple green salad. This goes well with Chicken Teriyaki, Pork Tonkatsu, or any other Japanese dish.

Makes 1/3 cup

Greek Salad Dressing*

2 tablespoons red wine vinegar
2 tablespoons extra virgin olive oil
3 tablespoons lemon juice
1 clove garlic, minced
½ teaspoon dried oregano
¼ teaspoon salt
¼ teaspoon pepper

Combine ingredients and whisk together until well blended. Serve over a salad of romaine lettuce, tomatoes, cucumbers, kalamata olives and thinly sliced red onion. Top with feta cheese.

*Make this dressing at least 2 hours before you serve it. Keep it at room temperature. The ingredients will blend together and the flavor will improve. The longer it sets, the better it gets.

Makes ¼ cup

Honey Mustard Dressing

¼ cup honey
3 tablespoons Dijon mustard
1 tablespoon vinegar
3 tablespoons extra virgin olive oil
Juice of ½ lemon
Salt and pepper

Whisk honey, mustard, vinegar, olive oil, and lemon juice together until well blended. Add salt and pepper to taste. It's so delicious, it tastes good on anything.

Makes ½ cup

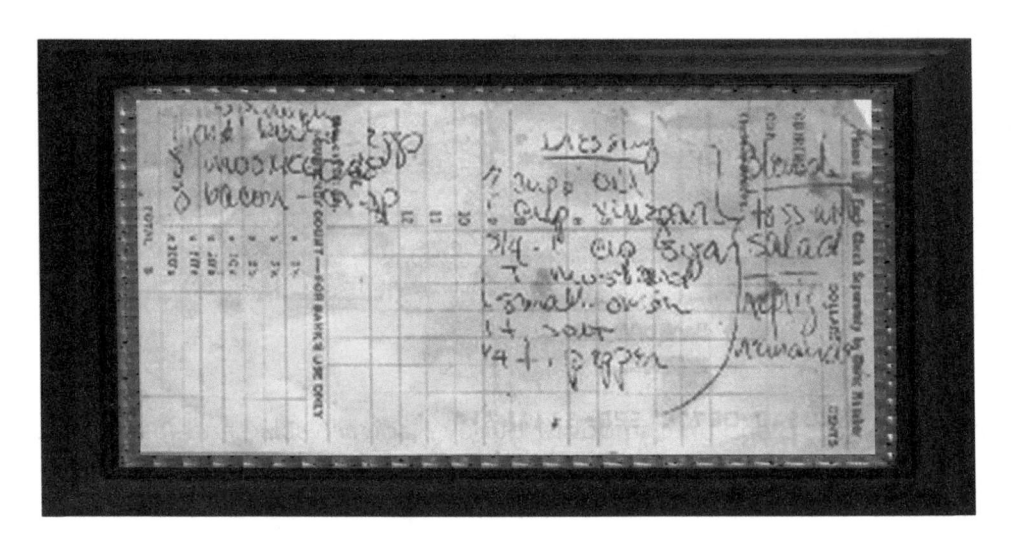

The check stub/recipe card for Spinach Salad Dressing
The Crepes and Cream salad dressing lives on, thanks to a grocery store produce manager.

Spinach Salad Dressing

From 1974 to 1979 my husband and I lived in Richmond, Virginia, with our two young children. On the weekend, we hired a sitter and treated ourselves to a night out on the town. It didn't matter what we did. Frankly, just being able to talk with people over the age of four was reward enough.

In addition to visiting with friends and going to movies, we enjoyed trying different restaurants in the area. One of our favorites was a small restaurant called Crepes and Cream located in nearby Midlothian. The food was good, the prices reasonable, and the atmosphere pleasant. What more could we ask?

Their menu featured crepes, of course, but had lots of other delightful choices. In addition to their wonderful asparagus, ham, and cheese crepe, my favorite thing to order was their signature spinach salad. It was a big old-fashioned spinach salad with the usual ingredients in it—mushrooms, hard-boiled eggs, bacon, and croutons.

What made this salad so special was the dressing. It was a fairly light dressing with a blend of sweet and pungent flavors. I never could figure out what was in it, but it was addictive. It was the perfect dressing for spinach salad.

I'll never forget the day when the great salad dressing mystery was solved. I was shopping at a grocery store near the restaurant, and there it was. Taped above the fresh spinach in the produce section was a handwritten copy of the Crepes and Cream spinach salad dressing recipe. It was a dream come true.

I quickly wrote down the elusive ingredients on the only piece of paper I had - the back of a check stub. That's exactly how it's remained in my recipe box ever since.

Crepes and Cream closed after several years, but their salad dressing lives on, all because of a creative grocery store produce manager. Thanks, whoever you are!

Spinach Salad Dressing

1 cup vegetable oil
1/2 cup vinegar
1/2 cup sugar
1 teaspoon Dijon mustard
1/2 small onion, minced
1/2 teaspoon salt
Dash pepper

Put ingredients in blender. Blend until smooth. Pour over spinach salad and toss gently.

Makes 1 ¾ cups

Spinach Salad*

1/2 pound fresh spinach, torn into bite sized pieces
1/2 pound bacon, fried and crumbled
8 oz. package mushrooms, sliced
6 hard boiled eggs, sliced
Croutons (See recipe below)

Mix salad ingredients in a large bowl and toss with dressing. Top with croutons.

*This is the traditional spinach salad recipe, but you can add additional ingredients if you like. I like to add cherry tomatoes, mandarin orange segments, dried cranberries, and some red onion slices for color contrast and extra flavor.

Serves 6

Croutons

½ French baguette, cut into ½ inch cubes
3 tablespoons olive oil
Sea salt
Freshly ground pepper

Heat olive oil in a large skillet over medium heat. When the oil is hot, add the bread cubes and sprinkle with a little salt and pepper. Reduce the heat and stir frequently so that bread is toasted well on all sides. Sprinkle with a little more salt and pepper. The bread cubes should be lightly browned and crispy.

Remove from pan and let cool. Use as many as you like in the salad and save the rest in an airtight container to use in other salads and soups.

SOUPS

Garnish the rabbit ears with tin foil and watch the test pattern

Cream of Celery Soup

I know exactly when I began to love a good hot bowl of soup. I was in junior high school. One of my favorite television shows was "Lassie". Campbell's Soup sponsored this show about a loving family, their son Timmy, and their heroic dog, Lassie. It was right then and there, during those commercials, that I began to crave soup. If Timmy's mother served him soup, I wanted some too.

There's no doubt that television has a powerful affect on the viewer. We got our first TV in 1955, when I was in the fifth grade. From that point on, our family was forever changed. We gathered around the set in the evening, rearranging the "rabbit ears" (antenna) for better reception. We even put wads of tin foil on them because it was supposed to improve the picture. This sounds positively primitive now, but it was common practice then.

NBC, ABC, and CBS were the only channels. When they weren't on, or there were "technical difficulties," a test pattern (NBC had a peacock), would appear on the screen. At midnight, the National Anthem was played, and the test pattern appeared until the next morning when programming resumed.

Rich people had color television. Their peacock was a stunning array of primary colors. We had a black and white TV. Our peacock was grey and black.

I can remember the commercials almost as well as the shows. These commercials made us want to see the U.S.A. in a Chevrolet, use Texaco gas, brush our teeth with Ipana toothpaste, and buy Swanson T.V. dinners. In my case, I suddenly had to have Campbell's soup.

The canned soup choices were fairly limited in the 1950s. Mother usually had tomato, vegetable, cream of mushroom, and chicken noodle soup in the pantry. I loved them all. I don't remember celery soup being in there, however. I must have discovered cream of celery soup somewhere between the Lassie years and American Bandstand era. It doesn't really matter when I first tasted it. The point is that it became an instant favorite.

I found a recipe for this delicious soup and want to share it. I'm pretty sure you're going to love it as much as I do. The recipe contains both celery and celery root, which I found interesting. Celery root, also known as celeriac, is a knobby looking vegetable. It's not very attractive on the outside but has a wonderful celery flavor on the inside.

This recipe is simple, easy, and a cinch for the novice cook. Turn on some old television shows, have a nice bowl of celery soup, and relax. If you're really lucky, you might catch a rerun of "Lassie".

Cream of Celery Soup

1 small celery root, peeled and diced
1 medium onion, chopped
6 stalks of celery, (with leafy tops), thinly sliced
4 cups low sodium chicken broth
Salt
Freshly ground pepper
1/3 cup cream or half and half
1/4 cup chopped fresh chives (optional)

Rinse the celery root. Cut away the outer part, and dice the inside. Combine the onion, celery, celery root and broth in a large saucepan. Bring to a boil, reduce heat, cover, and simmer until the celery root is completely tender and breaks apart when pierced by a fork (about 25 minutes).

Cool the soup a little before putting half of it into a food processor or blender. Blend until smooth.

Repeat with second half. Return the soup to the saucepan and season with salt and pepper to taste. Stir in the cream or half and half.

Garnish with fresh chives, if you like.

Serves 4

The "Tomato Man" at the Charlotte, North Carolina, Farmer's Market
Vegetables so fresh they're in the garden in the morning and on the dinner table by evening.

Garden Fresh Vegetable Soup

When I was growing up, summer was that wonderfully lazy time between Memorial Day and Labor Day. Our days were spent playing hide-and-go-seek and kick-the-can, running barefoot by day, and catching lightning bugs at night. It was a time for sleeping late, reading books, attending summer camp, and going to the local swimming pool. It was also time for enjoying the delicious vegetables from my father's garden.

Daddy loved working in the soil and always had a plot of land somewhere close-by for his garden. During the summer, we were treated to fresh limas, cucumbers, tomatoes, peas, corn, squash, green beans, and watermelon. It was heavenly. I can still picture Daddy sitting on the porch shelling peas, just as happy as he could be.

I don't garden but love people who do. I've found that the closest thing to having your own garden is to shop at a local farmer's market. I love everything about a good farmer's market—the smell of the vegetables, the down-to-earth people who sell their crops, the hum of the bees, the homemade pies, cakes, and jellies for sale, the fresh flowers and herbs available, the corn that was "just picked this morning", the produce that changes as the seasons do, and yes, even the dirt that still clings to some of the vegetables.

I love to go to the farmer's market in the morning, load up the car with fresh vegetables, and come home and cook them in the afternoon. My father would love the idea of vegetables that were in the garden in the morning and on the dinner table by evening. It just doesn't get any fresher than that.

130

One of my favorite things to make after a morning at the farmer's market is called Garden Fresh Vegetable Soup. I usually make a big pot and can some of it. It's awesome served hot in the middle of February. You can enjoy it now – or later.

Try serving this soup chilled, with crusty French bread and a small green salad. It's the perfect light lunch for a hot summer day.

Garden Fresh Vegetable Soup

4 large tomatoes
1 ½ cup canned low sodium chicken broth
4 scallions, thinly sliced
1 small cucumber, sliced
1/2 cup diced green pepper
1 cup low sodium V-8 juice
Juice of 1 lemon
2 teaspoons sugar
1 tablespoon salt
1/4 teaspoon freshly ground pepper
Fresh chives, chopped (optional)

Peel and chop tomatoes. In a large saucepan, simmer scallions, cucumber, green pepper, and tomatoes in chicken broth for 5 minutes. Add tomato juice, lemon juice, sugar, salt, and pepper. Simmer, covered, for 10 minutes. Serve chilled. Garnish with fresh chopped chives, if desired.

Joy's First Solo Sleigh Ride—The Winter of 1947
After she crashed into a snow bank on the first run, her dreams of Olympic bobsledding were over.

Winter Tomato Soup

I'm one of those people who really likes wintertime. I don't mind being cold, and actually find a blustery winter day invigorating. Because I grew up in the mountains of Virginia, and lived in New York for almost twenty years, cold weather and snow don't faze me.

I associate so many happy childhood activities with winter—sleigh riding, ice skating, and making snowmen, snow angels, and snow ice cream, for example. I loved coming home to a mug of hot chocolate and the aroma of soup simmering on the stove. I really like that warm snuggly feeling of being safely inside while the weather rages outside.

Now that we live in South Carolina, there's not a whole lot of raging winter weather going on, but occasionally we do get a real honest-to-goodness snowstorm. These snows are infrequent, but welcome by me.

It was during one of these rare snow days that I met my husband for lunch. I ordered tomato soup and a grilled cheese sandwich. So did he. Looking around the restaurant, I realized that most of the other customers had done the same thing.

The woman who took our order said she had never seen anything like it. Everybody was ordering the tomato soup and a grilled cheese sandwich. It really shouldn't have come as a surprise, though. There's an irresistible urge to want this combination when the weather's cold.

A good hot bowl of tomato soup, accompanied by a crunchy grilled cheese sandwich, is absolutely my favorite cold weather meal. Therein lies the problem.

I like real fresh tomato soup, which as we all know, is basically impossible to find in the dead of winter. Strangely enough, it was in the heat of the summer that I came across a solution to this problem.

I attended a luncheon at a friend's home, and she served a delicious tomato soup. It was so good I assumed it was fresh from the garden. I asked for the recipe, and was shocked to find that it was made using canned tomatoes.

Not until months later when I was making this recipe did I have one of those "light bulb moments". This could be my winter tomato soup. And so it is.

Next time the weather is cold and miserable, treat yourself to a bowl of this wonderful tomato soup. Fix yourself a crispy gooey grilled cheese sandwich to go with it, and think of me. I'll be having the same thing.

Winter Tomato Soup

1/2 cup chopped onions
3 tablespoons butter
3 tablespoons flour
1 cup chicken broth
28 ounce can Italian-style tomatoes
3 tablespoons tomato paste
1 tablespoon chopped parsley
1 tablespoon sugar
1 teaspoon salt
1/2 teaspoon dried basil
1/4 teaspoon pepper
1 bay leaf
Cream (optional)
Fresh basil

In a large saucepan, sauté onions in butter until tender. Add flour, stirring until smooth. Gradually stir in broth and cook over medium heat until it thickens. Add tomatoes, and the next 7 ingredients, and bring to a boil. Cover, reduce heat, and simmer 30 minutes. Remove bay leaf.

Put half of the mixture into a food processor, and blend until smooth. Return to sauce pan. Repeat procedure with remaining mixture.

Serve in bowls, stirring in a little cream if desired. Garnish with fresh basil.

Serves 4

The seemingly endless dog days of summer are finally over, and I regain my will to live.

Old Virginia Beef Stew

There's a defining day every year when you know that fall has officially arrived. You step out the door in the morning, and there's an unmistakable difference in the air. It's crisp and cool, the sky is clear, and the humidity has totally disappeared.

This is, without a doubt, my favorite time of the year. The seemingly endless dog days of summer are finally over, and I regain my will to live. I feel energized and happy, ready to take on almost anything.

I pull my tennis racket out of the hall closet and head off to the courts for the first time in three months. I tackle yard work with renewed vigor, weeding my herb garden and the horribly neglected and overgrown flower beds.

It's time to buy chrysanthemums to put out on the front steps and to decorate the house for fall. My pumpkin centerpiece goes on the kitchen table, the autumn flag is hangs outside, and all's right with the world.

I have no idea why, but I suddenly develop a craving for beef stew in the fall. I guess the chill in the air triggers a need for a good hearty meal. As far as I'm concerned, there's nothing better to satisfy this need than a big pot of stew.

My husband loves beef stew and swore by "Dinty Moore Beef Stew" for years. He and "Dinty Moore" spent quite a bit of time together in the early days of our marriage.

I found a gem of a recipe for beef stew in an old cookbook of my mother's. The recipe, called Old Virginia Beef Stew, is as good as it gets. A bowl of this stew is wonderfully robust and just plain good for the soul. I think that it's the perfect way to celebrate the cool crisp days of autumn. Happy days are here again!

Old Virginia Beef Stew *

1 pound stew beef, cut in 1 inch cubes
3 tablespoons oil (I use olive oil)
5 cups hot water
1 chopped onion
Juice of 1 lemon
1 1/2 teaspoons salt
1/2 teaspoon pepper
1/2 teaspoon paprika
1/2 teaspoon allspice
1 teaspoon sugar
1 tablespoon Worcestershire sauce
2 cups tomato juice
1 cup sliced carrots
1 cup diced celery
1 cup cubed potatoes

Brown meat in oil. Add 3 cups water, onion, lemon juice, seasonings, Worcestershire sauce and 1 cup tomato juice. Simmer for 2 hours. Add remaining 2 cups of water and 1 cup of tomato juice before adding carrots and celery. Simmer for 1 hour. Add potatoes, and cook for another 30 minutes. Serve.

* I sometimes add other vegetables to this basic recipe, such as a can of diced tomatoes, a can of green beans (drained, and beans cut in half), and a can of corn (drained). These additions make this dish more like a beef vegetable soup than a stew.

Joy modeling her new Easter bonnet in front of the church – Easter 1946
We sang lots of hymns with "Alleluia" in them and had a ham dinner that afternoon.

Delicious Bean Soup

Easter holds many special memories for me. Growing up in Roanoke, Virginia, I knew that Easter was approaching when Agnew's seed store on the market had real bunnies, ducks and little chicks in the window. Believe it or not, the chicks were dyed in pretty pastel colors. Weird, but true.

It was time to dye Easter eggs and to get new clothes for church. It was time for Easter egg hunts, chocolate bunnies, and jelly beans. It was a great time to be a kid.

On Easter morning, my brother and I searched for our baskets full of candy and eggs that the Easter Bunny had left for us. We went to church and sang lots of hymns with "Alleluia" in them and had a ham dinner that afternoon.

My mother's ham was something to behold. She scored the skin in a diamond pattern, sticking cloves in each juncture, and basted it with a brown sugar glaze. It looked pretty, smelled great, and tasted even better.

With the ham hock, she made a wonderful bean soup called Senate Bean Soup. This soup was served in the U.S. Senate dining room, according to the recipe.

This must have been THE recipe for bean soup back then, because everybody made it. The soup was good all by itself, but my grandmother always added a spoonful of catsup and relish to hers before eating it. I followed her lead and learned to love it that way.

I still stir some catsup and relish into my bowl of bean soup, even though my husband thinks it's gross. I just don't do it in front of him. It's sort of the "Don't ask, don't tell" approach to eating bean soup, which seems to work for us.

Years ago, on a trip to Pennsylvania Dutch country, I ate the most delicious bean soup I've ever had. It was similar to Senate Bean Soup, but I liked it better. I asked the waitress for the recipe, and much to my surprise, she gave it to me. The soup is aptly named "Delicious Bean Soup".

If you're celebrating Easter with a ham dinner, try making this soup with your leftovers. Sneak a little catsup and relish into it at your own risk—just don't let my husband see you do it.

Delicious Bean Soup

1 pound dried navy beans
2 1/2 quarts water
1 meaty ham bone (1 1/2 pounds)
1 clove garlic, minced
1 bay leaf
1 cup cubed potatoes
1 cup celery, sliced
1 cup onion, finely chopped
1 cup carrots, sliced
Salt, pepper*

Sort and rinse the beans. Boil the beans in water for 2 minutes, and remove from heat. Cover, and let stand for 1 hour. Add the ham bone, garlic, and bay leaf to the beans. Simmer, covered, for 2 hours or until the beans are almost tender. Add the potatoes and vegetables and more water if needed. Simmer for 1 hour.

Remove the ham hock, cut the meat from the bone, dice it, and add it to the soup. (Add more diced ham if desired.) Remove the bay leaf and season soup with salt and pepper to taste.

*For more flavor, I add a couple of ham bouillon cubes to the soup.

Taking hungry children to NYC? Save your sanity. Find a street vender – Quick!

Chilled Cherry Soup

My husband and I, with our two small children, ages five and three, moved to New York in 1979 from Richmond, Virginia. We stayed there for almost twenty years.

We lived twenty miles north of New York City on the Hudson River, in the village of Sleepy Hollow. It is the smallest town we've lived in, yet it is part of one of the largest metropolitan areas in the world. We were never at a loss for things to do with the children.

We went ice-skating at Rockefeller Center, rode elephants at the Bronx Zoo, stood at the top of the World Trade Center, toured museums, stood in the cold to watch the Macy's Thanksgiving Day Parade, saw the Rockettes perform at Radio City Music Hall, and attended Broadway plays.

The Empire State Building, the Statue of Liberty, China Town, and the Central Park Zoo were soon on our "been there, done that" list. We saw the Yankees and the Mets play, attended the U.S. Open tennis tournament, the Westchester Classic P.G.A. golf tournament, and went to West Point to see Army football games.

One of the things we quickly learned about taking children into the city is that the food for sale on the street is where the action is. New York City street food is one of the best-kept secrets in town. It's good, plentiful, convenient, and comparatively cheap.

138

Hot dogs, big pretzels, and ice cream were abundant, but other common choices included shish kebab, sausage and peppers, bratwurst, and Italian ices. The roasted chestnuts available at Christmastime were my favorite. They still are.

The most unique thing I ever had was fruit soup. My daughter Whitney and I went into the city one hot summer day and spotted a vendor selling chilled soups. We were intrigued by a beautiful pink soup with whole blueberries floating in it. Not only was it gorgeous, it was terrific. Right there on the sidewalk in New York, we had one of our best lunches ever.

I forgot all about this wonderful soup until years later when a friend served chilled cherry soup at a luncheon. It looked familiar. It was pink and had blueberries floating in it. I was delighted to find that it was similar to what Whitney and I had eaten for lunch so many years ago on the streets of Manhattan. My friend gave me her recipe, and I've been making it ever since.

Serve this chilled as a first course, or as a main dish summer soup. If you want to have an authentic New York City experience, go outside and eat it on the sidewalk.

Chilled Cherry Soup

3 cups sweet cherries, pitted
1/2 cup bottled cherry juice
1 teaspoon grated orange rind
1/2 cup fresh orange juice (about 1 orange)
1/3 cup low fat sour cream
1/3 cup plain fat free yogurt
1/4 cup sugar
Fresh blueberries for garnish

Put all ingredients, except blueberries, in a blender. Blend until smooth. Chill.

Serve chilled, topped with fresh blueberries.

Joy and Bonnie—Age 3
"Yes, we're twins, but we're not identical."

Vichyssoise

My cousin Bonnie is one month younger than I am, and we look nothing alike. As kids, she was blonde with blue eyes, and I was a brown-eyed brunette. We're both adopted, so there's not even a chance of a faint family resemblance.

Our mothers were sisters and delighted in dressing us alike when we were little. Even though Bonnie grew up in Ednor, Maryland, and I lived in Roanoke, Virginia, we saw each other several times a year. In our look-alike clothes, we drew attention on outings with our mothers. People would ask us if we were twins and we answered with straight faces, "Yes, but we're not identical."

I have fond memories of my trips to Maryland to visit Bonnie. I vividly remember many of the places our mothers took us in and around Washington, D.C. We went shopping at department stores like Garfinkles, Woodward and Lothrop, and Jelleff's, now long gone. Those were the days when you actually got dressed up to go shopping—I'm talking dresses, petticoats, and patent leather shoes dressy.

After we shopped, we had lunch at a nice restaurant. The one I remember most was Mrs. K's Toll House Tavern, in Silver Spring, Maryland. It was fancy enough that we knew to sit up straight and use our best table manners.

Lunch there was a leisurely event, and the food was excellent. It was there that I tasted vichyssoise for the first time. I learned a lot that day. I didn't know that people ate cold soup on purpose, but they do. I found out that this chilled soup is not only refreshing but also creamy and really good.

Since that day, whenever I see vichyssoise on a menu, I order it and think of Mrs. K's Toll House Tavern and two little girls having a dressed up lunch with their mothers.

I was having lunch with a friend recently and the subject of vichyssoise came up. I began to wax nostalgic about the first time I ever ate it. Several days later, I got a neatly printed recipe for this wonderful soup in the mail. A coincidence? I think not.

The good news is that, other than having a really thoughtful friend, the recipe is fabulous. I'm going to be sure to share it with my cousin Bonnie.

Vichyssoise

3 large leeks, rinsed and sliced (white part only)
1 small onion, chopped
1 celery stalk, chopped
1 tablespoon butter
2 large baking potatoes, cut into bite size cubes
Two (14 ounce) cans low sodium chicken broth
White pepper
Salt
1 cup cream or half and half
Fresh chives, chopped

Sauté leeks, onions, and celery in butter until soft, not brown, about five minutes. Add potatoes and chicken broth. Bring to a boil, reduce heat, and simmer, covered, for about 20 minutes, until the potatoes are soft.

Puree in blender, adding some more liquid if it's too thick. Add salt and pepper to taste. Cover and chill for several hours (overnight is best). Stir in cream and serve. Garnish with chopped fresh chives.

Serves 4

Aside from the turkey, if it doesn't come from a box or a can, my family is suspicious.
Photograph courtesy of the Fort Mill Times

Butternut Squash Soup

Because I love to cook I really enjoy Thanksgiving. I love every aspect of it. After all, I learned from the master—my mother. Mother was an excellent cook and an accomplished hostess. She loved to entertain and it showed.

For example, our Thanksgiving table was exquisite. A beautiful centerpiece, usually a cornucopia overflowing with fruit and nuts, flanked by candles and fall flowers, set the stage. It was picture perfect. Fortunately I have Mother's things so I'm able to set a similar table, which makes me happy.

Mother had a tradition of placing three pieces of dried corn in front of our plates. It was to remind us of the hardships suffered by the Pilgrims during their first winter in America. Before we ate, each of us would share three things for which we were thankful. It was literally a way to count our blessings. I've continued this family tradition with my children, minus the corn. My hope is that they'll want to carry it on with their families.

As for our meal, it was always predictable. Turkey, rice, gravy, green beans, oyster dressing, sweet potato casserole with marshmallows on top, cranberry sauce, pumpkin bread, and pie for dessert.

My family is predictable too. My husband and children are very different—wonderful, but different. They are afraid of anything new. Aside from the turkey, if it doesn't come from a box or a can they're suspicious. It's somehow comforting to them to see the empty containers on the counter. If the cranberry sauce isn't in the shape of a can, complete with the little circular ridges on it, they're not interested. I can't make this stuff up.

Imagine their reaction when I served butternut squash soup one year for the first course. I served it in a big pumpkin shaped tureen that looked great on the table next to my mother's cornucopia. To my surprise, they were impressed by the tureen and tried the soup. It was actually a big hit. Who knew?

This delicious soup has earned a permanent place on our Thanksgiving menu. The good news is that you can make it ahead of time. It keeps well in the refrigerator. Just heat and serve.

Try introducing this dish to your family. If they're like mine, bringing it to the table in a pumpkin shaped soup tureen might not be a bad idea.

Butternut Squash Soup

1 butternut squash
2 cups low sodium chicken broth
½ teaspoon cinnamon plus enough to garnish
¼ teaspoon nutmeg
¼ cup honey
1 cup cream (I substitute half and half)

Cut the squash in half long-ways. Scoop out the seeds. Place flat side down on a greased baking dish. Bake at 350 degrees for 45 minutes. Cool. Remove skin.

Place half of the pulp in a blender or food processor with 1 cup of chicken broth. Blend until smooth. Pour mixture in a large saucepan. Repeat the process with the other half of the squash and the remaining chicken broth. Add to saucepan. Simmer on low heat until warm. Add the cinnamon, nutmeg, and honey to the soup, stirring well. Add cream then stir and simmer for 10 minutes.

Ladle into bowls. Sprinkle a little cinnamon on top and serve.

Serves 4-6.

BREADS

MARVIN SMITH

JIM NOLAND

ATO Concession Managers 1964–1966
One became a businessman, the other a Methodist minister.

ATO Beer Bread

My husband Marvin grew up as an only child in a lower income family. They didn't have enough money to send him to college.

Marvin stood out as an excellent student in high school. Marvin's French teacher, Madame Falwell, was determined that he deserved a chance to further his education. She felt so strongly about this that she wrote an impassioned letter to the president of the University of Virginia, insisting that Marvin be admitted and offered a scholarship.

Not only was he admitted, he was also given a full scholarship. He had to earn his own spending money, however. That's when things got interesting. One summer he worked as a bank teller, and the following summer he worked as a clerk at an ABC store. Both jobs provided him with some of the money he needed and some unique experiences.

Marvin's other job was the most memorable. He was a member of the ATO fraternity and took over the concession management during his third and fourth years at school. What this means is that he ran the bar. He and another fraternity brother, Jim Noland, bought beer for 18 cents a can, and sold it for 25 cents a can. Sheer volume made this a profitable business and covered his college expenses.

Marvin and Jim learned valuable lessons about running the bar. Never buy Old Milwaukee beer. The guys refused to drink it. Always buy Pabst Blue Ribbon beer (aka – PBR). None was ever left over. It was the gold standard by which all other beers were judged.

Marvin became a businessman and Jim became a Methodist minister, but for two years, these guys were extraordinary beer salesmen.

I remember those days well because I was dating Marvin at the time. Every time I drink a PBR, I'm reminded of good times at the ATO house seeing Marvin behind the bar, listening to the bands that played the rock and roll music of the 60s, and hanging out with his fraternity brothers.

Recently I went to a dinner party where everyone brought a dish to share. One guest brought a warm loaf of buttered beer bread that was great. As I enjoyed it, I had a stroke of genius – what if I made this bread and used PBR as the beer? It would be ATO bread!

I'm not much of a baker but decided to make an exception in this case. The bread turned out great. It's especially delicious when paired with songs like "Shout!", "My Girl," and "Double Shot of my Baby's Love." From the ATO house to yours, I give you beer bread. You're going to love it—especially if you've got a nice cold glass of PBR handy.

ATO Beer Bread *

3 cups self-rising flour
3 tablespoons sugar
1 egg (room temperature)
12 oz. PBR beer (room temperature)
¼ cup melted butter

Mix flour and sugar together. Beat egg and beer together in a large bowl. Add flour and sugar into the beer mixture and stir until the two are combined.

Pour into a greased loaf pan and bake at 350 degrees for 45 minutes. Brush crust with butter 5 minutes before it is done. Serve warm.

* This bread isn't pretty like traditional loaves, but don't judge it by its looks. This dense bread goes well with robust soups and stews. ATO beer bread is the perfect accompaniment to your corned beef and cabbage dinner on St. Patrick's Day—with a PBR, of course!

Serves 8-10

Miss Mattox—1958
When letters replaced numbers, things went downhill in a hurry.

No Brainer Braided Loaf

Just because I like to cook, people assume that baking is one of my specialties. They're wrong. Baking requires exact measurements of ingredients or the recipe is ruined. Exact measurements sometime require simple math skills when doubling or dividing a recipe. It's a widely known fact that I have no math skills. None.

I distinctly remember the exact moment when I lost touch with math. It was in Miss Mattox's sixth period algebra class at Woodrow Wilson Junior High School. Miss Mattox wrote the letter x on the blackboard. Then she wrote the letter y. When letters replaced numbers, things went downhill in a hurry.

From that moment on, I was doomed to years in summer school taking remedial math classes with the football team in order to pass.

College math was no different. There was still an unknown factor that eluded me. Much to everyone's surprise (including mine), after four years of math classes, I got the two credits I needed to graduate. Then I moved on to my post math life.

I am happy to report that I have never needed to find x or y in the real world, nor have I heard of anyone who was looking for them.

All was going smoothly until I tried to bake something. Suddenly, it was necessary to know what 1/2 of 3/4 was in order to cut down a recipe. This was not good. Where was Miss Mattox when I needed her?

I used common sense instead of math to solve this problem. Eyeballing the measuring cup until it looked like half the amount worked just fine. That's my method, and I'm sticking to it.

My mother inadvertently solved my baking problem. On one of my trips home to visit my parents, Mother baked a fresh loaf of bread for dinner. It was hot, golden, and delicious. I was duly impressed and told her so. She laughed and shared her secret with me. The loaf was made from frozen bread dough. She hadn't mixed or measured anything. This was an "ah ha" moment for me. Thus began the bread baking stage of my life.

My favorite recipe transforms a humble loaf of bread into a beautiful braided loaf with some surprise ingredients baked inside. You're going to love it.

If you don't have frozen dough, don't worry about it. Plan B is only as far away as the boxed mixes in the baking aisle. I know it well.

No Brainer Braided Loaf

1 pound loaf frozen bread dough
3 tablespoons softened butter (not melted) plus 1 tablespoon melted butter
½ cup grated Parmesan cheese
2 teaspoons garlic salt
2 tablespoons instant minced onion
1 tablespoons dried Italian herbs
½ teaspoon paprika
Corn meal
Sesame seeds

Thaw bread dough in a greased loaf pan. Cover and let rise until doubled in size (about 3-6 hours). On a floured surface, roll the dough into a 13 x 11 inch rectangle. Spread 3 tablespoons of butter on the dough. Sprinkle cheese, garlic salt, minced onion, herbs, and paprika evenly over the butter. Fold the 13-inch sides to the center, overlapping them about 1 inch. Press the center down to seal. With the seam side up, transfer to a greased baking sheet sprinkled with corn meal.

Make diagonal cuts 1 inch apart on each side of the rectangle to within 1 inch of the center. Fold opposite strips across each other at an angle, alternating from side to side to give a crisscross appearance. Pinch ends to seal. Brush with melted butter and sprinkle with sesame seeds. Let rise until doubled in bulk (about 1 hour). Bake at 350 degrees for 20-25 minutes.

I remember the parade, the chill in the air, the exciting rivalry, and the roar of the crowd.

Thanksgiving Pumpkin Bread

Thanksgiving is one of my favorite holidays. I love everything associated with it—food, fellowship, family, friends, a fire in the fireplace, and, yes, football on TV. It just doesn't get any better than that, as far as I'm concerned.

Thanksgiving never fails to bring back warm, happy, childhood memories of this special day. In my hometown of Roanoke, Virginia, there was a football game on Thanksgiving Day between V.M.I. (Virginia Military Institute) and V.P.I. (Virginia Polytechnic Institute, known these days as Virginia Tech). The game, known as the "Military Classic of the South," was played from 1913 to 1969. The V.M.I. Keydets and the V.P.I. Cadet Corps met at the train station in the morning, and marched through town to Victory Stadium, about three miles away. It was quite a spectacle.

This great college rivalry evoked deep loyalties in us at an early age. Even in elementary school, we knew who was for V.M.I. or V.P.I. My best friend's father went to V.M.I., so naturally I became a Keydet fan. We actually dressed up to go to the game in those days, believe it or not, and wore ribbon corsages in the colors of our chosen school. My ribbons were, of course, red, white, and yellow to show my allegiance to V.M.I.

I remember the parade, the excitement of the game, the sweet aroma of my father's pipe tobacco, the chill in the air, the cheerleaders, and the roar of the crowd. It was magical.

No matter how exciting the game was, making things even better was the knowledge that after it was over, we were going home for Thanksgiving dinner. Coming into our house after the game was awesome. The aroma of a turkey dinner cooking in the oven has a powerful effect on cold, hungry football fans, that's for sure.

We knew there would be something for everyone at dinner. There would be oyster dressing for my brother, rice and gravy for me, and green beans cooked with a ham hock for my father. Aside from these mandatory dishes, we had stuffing, sweet potato casserole, cranberry sauce, pumpkin bread, and usually pecan pie for dessert.

I have most of Mother's Thanksgiving recipes but not the one for pumpkin bread. She probably loaned it to a friend and never got it back. It was officially lost. I tried some recipes, but they just weren't the same. Thanksgiving dinner didn't seem complete without that bread.

The good news is that our son solved the problem. He came home from a neighbor's house raving about the pumpkin bread they served. I immediately got the recipe and tried it. It turns out that our neighbor's pumpkin bread was a dead ringer for my mother's. The search was over. That delicious bread is now on our Thanksgiving table again. For that, I am truly grateful.

Thanksgiving Pumpkin Bread

3 1/2 cups sifted flour
3 cups sugar
1 1/2 teaspoons cinnamon
1 teaspoon baking powder
1 teaspoon allspice
1/2 teaspoon ground cloves
1/2 teaspoon nutmeg
2 teaspoons baking soda
1 1/2 teaspoons salt
3/4 cup water
1 cup oil
4 eggs
2 cups pumpkin
1 cup chopped nuts (optional)

Sift dry ingredients together. Make a well in the center and add other ingredients. Pour batter into 3 greased loaf pans and bake at 350 degrees for 1 hour. Baste with melted butter about 15 minutes before done. Let stand 10 minutes. Remove from pan to cool.

Makes 3 loaves. If you want to divide this recipe to make one or two loaves, you're on your own to do the math. I have no idea how to do it.

Aunt Ruby and Uncle John at the farm in Crewe, Virginia
The cornbread must be in the oven or she wouldn't be outside playing with the chickens.

Good Old Southern Cornbread

Cornbread is a distinctly southern dish. I know this for sure because my Aunt Ruby told me. If it had to do with food, especially southern food, Aunt Ruby was the expert.

Because Aunt Ruby and Uncle John lived on the Davis family farm in Crewe, Virginia, we visited them every summer. It gave my father a chance to visit his childhood home and relatives, and it gave the rest of us a chance to visit the farm.

I have vivid memories of my time spent there. I remember how bright the stars were at night in the country, the taste of cold spring water, being tucked into bed under one of my grandmother's quilts, the sound of rain on a tin roof, and the wonderful aromas coming from Aunt Ruby's kitchen. Her kitchen fascinated me.

The kitchen had a wood stove, as well as an electric stove. Aunt Ruby used both of them depending on what she was making. Breads and cakes came from the electric stove, while fried chicken and stew were cooked on the wood stove. The kitchen table was always covered with a flowery vinyl tablecloth. Because I was too short to reach my plate, Aunt Ruby put a big thick Sears and Roebuck catalog on my chair for me to sit on. Problem solved.

It was at Aunt Ruby's table that I ate my first cornbread. One afternoon I was lucky enough to be in the kitchen when she took some fresh cornbread out of the electric oven. She gave me a big slice and a glass of fresh buttermilk to go with it. I spread lots of butter on the cornbread and sprinkled salt on top of the buttermilk (I can't remember why). The combination of buttered cornbread and salted buttermilk just might be the best afternoon snack I've ever eaten.

I'd love to say I have Aunt Ruby's recipe for cornbread but I don't. I'm not even sure she had one. She just cooked things from memory without using exact measurements. She added a "pinch" of this and a "pat" of that as she cooked and things always came out perfectly. I'd love to know how she did it.

The good news is that recipes for cornbread are commonplace. No good southern cookbook would be complete without at least one recipe for cornbread—or corn pone, as Aunt Ruby sometimes called it. The bad news is that no two recipes are the same. Like barbeque sauce and chili, everyone seems to have their own version. I, too, have mine.

My recipe for cornbread has cheddar cheese and a touch of honey in it. I think these two ingredients make mine the best ever, except for Aunt Ruby's.

For authenticity, sit on an old Sears and Roebuck catalog at a table covered with a flowery vinyl tablecloth. Spread lots of butter on some warm cornbread and have a cold glass of buttermilk to go with it—sprinkled with salt, of course.

Good Old Southern Cornbread

1 stick butter
1 cup of cornmeal
1 cup all-purpose flour
1 tablespoon baking powder
1 egg
½ teaspoon salt
1 1/3 buttermilk
1 cup grated extra sharp cheddar cheese
1 tablespoon honey
Preheat oven to 400 degrees.

Put butter, cornmeal, flour, baking powder, egg, and salt in a food processor. Blend for 20-30 seconds. Add buttermilk, cheese, and honey and process for 15 seconds until thoroughly mixed.

Pour into a greased 8x8-inch pan and bake for 40 minutes. Cut into squares and serve warm.

Serves 6-8 people

BRUNCH, CHEESE AND SPREADS

Lois and Joy – "We told you breakfast was at 6 A.M. and you believed us!"

Lois's Breakfast Casserole

Breakfast is, without a doubt, my favorite meal of the day. That's the problem. I'm not a morning person, and for some unknown reason, most restaurants stop serving it by mid-morning. There are a handful of places that serve us sleepyheads all day long. God bless them!

I think Oscar Wilde was onto something when he said, "Only dull people are bright at breakfast." I'm convinced that society is made up of two groups of people—those who are bright at breakfast and those who aren't. I first noticed this in college. The first group walked briskly to the dining hall for breakfast on time, cheerful, chatty, fully dressed, and ready to greet the day. The rest of us trudged behind, silent, disheveled, and wearing trench coats over our nightgowns.

I'd like to say that I've outgrown this stage of my life, but I'd be lying. Friends know not to call me before 9 A.M. or to try to engage me in conversation requiring complete sentences before 10 A.M.

I was ecstatic when the concept of brunch became popular in this country. Combining breakfast and lunch is pure genius, bringing polar opposites to a common table.

I love everything about brunch and am a big fan of breakfast casseroles. Our friend, Lois Way, served one of my very favorite ones. She's quite the hostess and has served us many a delicious meal when we've stayed at her home. This one was a real home run.

This dish contains potatoes, cheese, scallions, bacon, and enough hot sauce to give it a little "kick". It's dainty enough for women, and hearty enough for the guys. It's the perfect combination.

What's even better is that you make it ahead of time. It's custom made for those of us who aren't morning people. All we have to do is take it out of the refrigerator, put it in the oven, and about 45 minutes later, eat.

I've served this casserole on Christmas morning for years now. It cooks while we're opening gifts and is ready for a festive breakfast when we are.

Got guests? Serve them something they'll all love. Even the groggy, incoherent ones will sit up, take notice, and ask for seconds.

Lois's Breakfast Casserole

12 ounces frozen Potatoes O'Brien, thawed
5 eggs
1/2 cup cottage cheese
1 cup shredded Monterey Jack cheese
2 chopped scallions
1 teaspoon salt
1/8 teaspoon pepper
4 dashes hot pepper sauce
6 slices bacon, cooked and crumbled*
Paprika

Lightly beat eggs in a large bowl. Stir in potatoes, cottage cheese, jack cheese, scallions, salt, pepper, and hot sauce. Turn into a buttered 10-inch pie plate. Scatter bacon over top and sprinkle with paprika. Cover with plastic wrap and refrigerate overnight.

Next morning place cold dish, uncovered, in a cold oven. Turn oven to 350 degrees and bake for 45 minutes, or until top is lightly brown and the casserole is firm in the middle. Cut in wedges, and serve.

Makes 6-8 servings

*Omit the bacon if you want. I do.

Mother makes her television debut. "Does being on television make me look fat?"

Mother's Granola

I remember exactly the first time my mother served some "new fangled" food called granola. It was July 6, 1968. My husband and I were visiting my parents at the time. When we came down to breakfast that morning, there it was, in a pretty bowl on the kitchen table next to the orange juice. It looked like some sort of crazy mixed-up cereal.

My husband, suspicious of anything new, took a pass on it. My father just looked amused, and ate his daily breakfast of bacon and eggs, without saying a word.

Mother cheerfully served some to me and I liked it. I REALLY liked it.

I don't know what inspired Mother to make granola. I don't know whether she went on a sudden health kick or just wanted to be on the cutting edge of the latest culinary trend, but I'm guessing the latter. Mother wasn't a tree-hugging, yoga-loving, health food nut. She was quite the opposite.

I'd love to know where she got her recipe, because it's a good one. She copied it down for me on a convenient piece of paper—the tear-off calendar page from that day, which is why I know exactly when I first tried it.

Today when I make Mother's granola, I still use that yellowed calendar page. It's pretty sad looking now, all folded and spattered, but her handwritten recipe is still legible and the granola is fantastic.

This recipe makes a big batch, but don't worry, it won't last long. My favorite way to enjoy granola is to eat it right out of the bowl. It's a great snack food. I also like it for breakfast with milk poured over it. Either way, it's delicious.

Mother's granola is chock full of good healthy ingredients, but you'd never know it. This might just be the perfect food. It's crunchy, sweet, AND good for you. Who knew? Who cares? Just enjoy.

Mother's Granola*

1 cup honey
1 cup oil
1 cup water
5 cups old-fashioned oatmeal
1 cup roasted peanuts
1 cup wheat germ
1 cup sunflower seed kernels
1 cup soy nuts
1 cup dry milk powder

Combine honey, oil, and water. Put all other ingredients in a large bowl. Pour liquid mix over the dry ingredients, and stir well.

Spread mixture over 3 flat pans (about 10 x 15 inch). Bake in a 275-degree oven for 1 hour, stirring every 15 minutes.

Let cool and store in tins.

* If you want to make it more like "trail mix", add dried fruit (cranberries, cherries, apricots, or raisins) right before serving.

Pull it out of the refrigerator, pop it into the oven, and "poof!", you've got a soufflé.

Overnight Cheese Souffle

Long before breakfast casseroles hit the scene, my mother fixed something she called Overnight Cheese Souffle. We had it for breakfast on special occasions—usually when company was visiting.

The beauty of this dish is its simplicity. It falls into the "Really Easy to Make" category. You actually assemble the souffle the night before you serve it. What could be easier?

In the morning, you pull this dish out of the refrigerator, pop it into the oven for 45 minutes to an hour before you want to eat, and *"poof!"*, you've got a soufflé—and a nice cheesy one at that. I promise that anyone can make this and look like a pro when it comes out of the oven.

Mother's cheese soufflé goes well with almost anything. Make it the centerpiece of your special breakfast or brunch, add a Bloody Mary or a Mimosa, and you're all set to celebrate. Cheers!

Overnight Cheese Souffle

8 slices of bread, crusts removed and cubed
½ pound extra sharp cheddar cheese, grated
5 eggs
2 cups of milk

1 teaspoon salt
1 scant teaspoon dry mustard
¼ cup butter, melted

In a greased 2 ½ -quart casserole dish alternate layers of bread cubes and cheese, ending with cheese on top. Beat eggs, and combine with milk, salt, and dry mustard. Pour over bread cubes and cheese. Cover, and refrigerate overnight.

When ready to bake, pour melted butter over the casserole. Bake at 350 degrees for 45-60 minutes. Place a loose piece of foil over the casserole to prevent it from browning too soon. Remove the foil for the last 15 minutes of baking.

Serve immediately.

Serves 4-6

I loved books so much that I read under the covers with a flashlight, long past my bedtime.

Heidi's Cheese Toast

As a child I spent a lot of time reading. I loved books so much that I read under the covers with a flashlight, long past my bedtime.

Two of my fictional friends had a huge impact on me early in life. The first was Dr. Seuss's character, Horton the elephant. My first and absolutely favorite book was "Horton Hatches the Egg". I renewed it so many times from the library that my parents finally bought me my own copy.

Horton's determination and courage intrigued me. I walked around quoting him all the time – "I meant what I said and I said what I meant, an elephant's faithful 100%". My parents must have been sick of it after a while.

I had the pleasure of meeting Dr. Seuss in 1986 at a book signing in New York City. He was promoting his new book, "You're Only Old Once". I stood in line to meet him with my copy of "Horton Hatches the Egg" tucked under my arm. When it was my turn, I told him about my love for Horton, and he smiled. He looked over my well-worn book and said, "Do you know this is a first edition?" I didn't. What I do know is that now I have a SIGNED first edition.

My second, and most influential, fictional friend was Heidi. Everything about her fascinated me. I wanted to be just like her—a little blonde girl who lived in the Swiss Alps in a cozy mountainside chalet with her grandfather, slept in a little alcove in a bed made of straw, and played with the goats.

I could only dream about these things, but there was one detail that became real to me. According to the story, when Heidi first arrived at her grandfather's rustic mountain home, he fixed her something to eat. He toasted some cheese over the fire and served it to her on bread with some warm milk.

Right away, cheese toast and warm milk became my new favorite meal. The warm milk phase faded pretty quickly, but my taste for cheese toast stuck with me. Even today, cheese toast rates right up there with my favorite foods.

In 1972, my husband and I traveled through the Swiss Alps and went to the top of Mt. Pilates. The view from the summit was stunning but a small chalet down the mountainside is what caught my eye. It looked like Heidi's house and I wasn't seeing it late at night under the covers with a flashlight! It was the real thing! A childhood dream come true.

Later that day at a small restaurant I ordered something that, roughly translated, was cheese toast. It was the best cheese toast ever. This recipe is about as close as possible to reliving that experience. Here's to Heidi, a mountain chalet, cheese toast, and a day in the Swiss Alps!

Heidi's Cheese Toast

2 slices rustic country bread about ½ inch thick
2 tablespoons butter, softened
¼ cup grated hard cheese (Asiago, Romano, Parmesan, Gruyere, or Provolone)
Sliced Kalamata olives (optional)
Minced sundried tomatoes (optional)
Tapenade (optional)
Pesto (optional)

Place the bread slices on a baking sheet. Spread with softened butter and sprinkle the cheese on top. Bake in a 400-degree oven for 10 minutes until the bread is crisp and the cheese is bubbly. Serve immediately.

For added flavor put olives or sundried tomatoes (or any ingredient you like – be creative!) on the buttered bread before topping with grated cheese. Bake as directed.

Substitute tapanade or pesto for the butter for a completely different version of cheese toast. Top with cheese and bake as directed.

Serves 2

Welsh Rarebit

Another cheese toast recipe I want to share with you originated in England. The English get a bad rap about their food being bland. This is just not true. When my husband and I visited London we had some great meals—especially in the pubs.

Our favorite was the Bayswater Arms Pub in Hyde Park. It took us a while to get used to the idea of "mushy peas" (literally mashed peas) with dinner and having baked beans for breakfast but other than that, the menu was loaded with good choices. The obligatory fish and chips was delicious, as were the crunchy potpies, the plump sausages and a nice variety of delicious cheeses.

You really must try the recipe below if you want to taste an English specialty. It's their version of cheese toast called Welsh Rarebit. I love it for lunch, accompanied by a good bowl of tomato soup, or served for brunch with eggs and bacon. The English get a big thumbs up for this yummy dish.

Welsh Rarebit

2 tablespoons butter
4 tablespoons beer
Salt and pepper to taste
1 cup shredded cheddar cheese
1 teaspoon spicy mustard
4 slices of bread, cut about ½ inch thick, toasted and buttered

Melt butter in a saucepan. Add the beer, salt, and pepper. Bring to the boiling point and add cheese and mustard. Stir just enough to melt the cheese. Do NOT bring to a boil.

Put the toast on a baking dish and pour the mixture over it. Place under the broiler, watching it carefully until the top is brown. Serve immediately.

Serves 4

First graders poised for the 100-yard dash to the cafeteria for competitive food swapping
(Joy is in the front row, 1st on the left)

Southern Style Pimento Cheese

Believe it or not, when I was growing up in Roanoke, Virginia, in the 1950s and early 1960s, there were no school buses. We walked to school—and liked it. We met our friends and walked together to our neighborhood schools. It was a social event.

Our elementary school, Virginia Heights Elementary, was only four blocks from my home. I have lots of vivid memories about my first school experience, especially eating in the cafeteria. Lunchtime there was not for the fainthearted. It was loud, the line to buy milk was long, and you had to move fast to get a seat with your friends. Once seated, you opened your lunch box, and the food swapping started.

Coveting your neighbor's lunch was the norm, and we quickly learned the art of negotiation. Some kids could skillfully swap their apple for someone else's Hershey bar before we even knew what happened. It was one of life's valuable lessons learned at an early age.

My lunchtime fare varied as I progressed through school. My peanut butter and jelly sandwich phase spanned my entire elementary school career. In junior high school, I ditched my Howdy Doody lunch box for a paper bag and began the bologna and cheese era of my life.

By the time I reached high school, I discovered the sophisticated taste of pimento cheese. It wasn't a passing fancy either, because I still love it.

I didn't realize how much I really liked pimento cheese until I moved to New York in 1979, and there was none at the grocery stores. Nobody even knew what it was, which was a real shock to me.

My friend, Jerrie Frye, came to the rescue by giving me her recipe for homemade pimento cheese. Quite honestly, it never occurred to me that I could actually make it myself. Instead of bootlegging pimento cheese to New York from Virginia as I had been, I started making my own.

I can't begin to tell you how much better Jerrie's recipe is than the commercial variety. Once you make it you'll never want any other kind. It's that good.

I recently asked some young moms if kids actually carry their lunches to school anymore and was delighted to find that they still do. I'd like to give a word of advice to these children—skip the peanut butter and jelly and the bologna and cheese, and go directly to the pimento cheese. You'll save yourself years of lackluster lunches this way. Also, be sure to give your mother this recipe.

Southern Style Pimento Cheese*

1 pound extra sharp cheddar cheese
1 small onion
4 oz. jar pimentos
¾ cup mayonnaise
Salt, pepper

Grate the cheese in a food processor. Take it out and set aside. Grate the onion in the processor. Drain the pimentos, and chop by hand. Add the cheese and the pimentos to the grated onion in the processor, and using the mixing blade, blend these ingredients. Add mayonnaise, a little at a time, and blend to the desired consistency. Add salt and pepper to taste.

Makes 2 cups

*For a breakfast treat, spread an English muffin with pimento cheese, and put it under the broiler until bubbly. It's also great as a stuffing for celery sticks. Try topping your hamburgers with pimento cheese instead of sliced cheese. I think you'll agree that it elevates the ordinary cheeseburger to a whole new level.

The Peaks of Otter – Picture courtesy of James Underwood
If you're looking for me I'm on top of the pointy one (Sharp Top) on the left.

Citrus and Spice Honey Spread

My husband and I enjoy staying at bed-and-breakfast inns. We've met some interesting people: the hosts, as well as the other guests.

The accommodations have ranged from rustic to magnificent. I've observed that the food usually, but not always, matches your surroundings. The fancier the house, the more elaborate the breakfast. A simple country home means good hardy fare. It's hard to go wrong either way.

We have some favorite B&Bs that we return to on a regular basis. One of these is an unpretentious home outside of Bedford, Virginia, with a stunning view of my favorite place on earth, the Peaks of Otter.

The owners of this B&B raise goats, keep bees, and have a chicken coop – complete with a boisterous rooster. Fortunately, the chicken coop is not within earshot of the house, so the crowing at dawn isn't an issue for the guests.

The breakfasts in their home are wholesome and delicious, with homemade jams and jellies, honey collected from the hives, and extremely fresh eggs. Now THAT'S a good breakfast.

For me, it's all about the honey. I love it. As far as I'm concerned, a nice fresh biscuit drizzled with honey is about as good as it gets, so I'm content there. I never leave without buying at least one jar of their honey.

After returning from one of our visits, I was inspired to find a good use for my new purchase. The best recipe I found was an incredibly simple one. The recipe, called Citrus and Spice Honey Spread, combines the honey with only two ingredients—grated orange zest and cinnamon. You won't believe how good it is when spread over a nice warm biscuit, a crusty roll, or an English muffin.

Having guests? Need a good addition to your breakfast or brunch table? Put a bowl of this delicious honey spread next to a basket of fresh bread and watch it disappear. How sweet it is!

Citrus and Spice Honey Spread

1 ¼ cups honey
2 ½ teaspoons finely grated orange zest
½ teaspoon ground cinnamon

Combine the ingredients into a bowl and stir to mix well. Spread over warm English muffins, biscuits, or rolls.

Makes 1 ¼ cups

One can never have too much honey

Honey Butter

I love honey. Always have. Always will.

When I was growing up, Mother always kept a product called Sioux Bee Honey Butter in the refrigerator. The container had a picture of a cute little Indian girl and a honeybee on the front of it. Why I remember this is anybody's guess.

Anyway, it wasn't the container I was interested in. It was the delicious concoction inside that was irresistible. The contents were thick like butter but sweet like honey. It was delicious when spread on toast, biscuits, or crackers.

I thought the honey butter tasted best when I sneaked it from the refrigerator, scooping up a dab of it on my finger. I thought no one would ever know. It never occurred to me that my mother could see my finger marks all over it. To her credit she never said a word.

For some inexplicable reason, Sioux Bee Honey Butter gradually disappeared. I don't remember when. I was probably in college when I realized it wasn't in the refrigerator anymore.

I'm delighted to report that I've learned how to make honey butter now. A friend gave me a recipe for it, and it's great. It's not exactly like Sioux Bee, but it's a close second.

At least it doesn't have fingerprints in it. Yet....

Honey Butter *

1 ¼ stick butter, softened
¼ cup honey
¾ cup confectioner's sugar

Whip ingredients with an electric mixer until smooth and spreadable. Store in a covered container in the refrigerator. It keeps well for a long time.

* Honey butter is the perfect addition to any brunch. Just put it on the table next to some hot biscuits or scones, and watch it disappear.

* As a snack, try dipping pretzels into honey butter. The sweet, salty combination is sinfully good. It's addictive. You'll go through a bag of pretzels in no time. A second bag of pretzels is optional.

Makes 2 cups

APPETIZERS

Virginia Beach – Summer of 1989
Blake serving "just caught from the pier" steamed crabs

Virginia Beach Crab Appetizer

I get nostalgic about one of the most delicious crustaceans on earth—crabs. My fondness goes back well into my childhood.

My Aunt Rena and Uncle Milton lived in Cape Anne, Maryland, about half a block from the Chesapeake Bay. We visited them in the summertime, as did many of my aunts, uncles, and cousins.

Whether they liked it or not, their home was a gathering place for family vacations. It was all about location, location, location. Sometimes we descended on them in droves, all sleeping in a dormitory style room upstairs in their one bedroom, one bath home.

In this large, unairconditioned room, I shared a bed with my cousin Bonnie. At night, we were surrounded by a symphony of snoring relatives who made sleeping difficult. Uncle Teddy's rhythmic grunting and whistling noises were the worst. The sleeping arrangements gave a whole new meaning to the term, "family closeness".

I remember that Cape Anne was a glorious place to visit. I spent my days there swimming at the small pier, running barefoot through the neighborhood, and fishing on Uncle Milton's boat. My cousins and I went crabbing together in the shallow water, walking carefully with our nets. After suffering a few pinched toes from the crabs, we quickly learned to wear our tennis shoes in the water during this risky activity.

There was nothing quite as satisfying as returning to the house with a pail of crabs. It was a proud moment. Aunt Rena steamed them, and everyone enjoyed an afternoon feast of fresh crabmeat.

Fortunately I was able to pass along the love of crabbing to my children. We vacationed at Virginia Beach every summer with the children, from the time they were in diapers until they left for college. Two of my college friends and their children joined us for this tradition.

The Virginia Beach pier was a perfect place for the children to spend a day crabbing. Some string, some chicken necks, a net, and a bucket entertained them for hours. Just as I had they proudly returned at the end of the day with a bucket of crabs. To quote Yogi Berra, "It was deja vu all over again." I steamed their catch and we enjoyed an afternoon feast of fresh crabmeat, thanks to the children.

I love crabs—whether they're deviled, soft shelled, or in bisque, dips, casseroles or cakes—it doesn't matter. They're all good.

One of my family's favorite recipes for crab is an appetizer I've served them ever since our son was born in 1973. I know this for sure, because on the back of this VERY tattered yellowed recipe, I found a list of scribbled questions to ask the pediatrician about our new infant.

I serve this appetizer on special occasions when we get together. It sparks happy memories for all of us. It's a great way to enjoy crab without getting your toes pinched!

Virginia Beach Crab Appetizer

6 ounces crab meat (canned is fine)
1 tablespoon (or more) fresh chopped parsley
1/4 cup minced onion
1 cup shredded cheddar cheese
3/4 cup mayonnaise
Party rye bread
Paprika

Mix ingredients well. Spread on party rye bread and sprinkle with paprika.

Put under broiler, until bubbly and beginning to brown. Watch carefully so it doesn't burn. Serve hot.

Serves 4-6

Linda Gerstman and Joy
Your guests will do an "about face" and ask for this recipe. Be nice like Linda. Give it to them.

Linda's Smoked Salmon Spread

My friend and former neighbor from New York, Linda Gerstman, gave me one of my favorite recipes. The recipe is for her smoked salmon spread, and it's fabulous.

We lived across the street from Linda and her husband Steve for almost 20 years in the village of Sleepy Hollow. Steve is a dentist with a seriously funny sense of humor. He's the type of dentist who would stuff a patient's mouth with cotton and then ask them a lot of unanswerable questions. He's known for his really stupid jokes, which he tells with relish. We've shared a lot of good times with the Gerstmans.

Linda is a great cook. I don't remember when or where she first served me her salmon spread, but I sure do remember my first taste. This was my introduction to lox and bagels. I probably did an instant "about face", said something like "Wow!" and asked for the recipe.

She graciously called the next day and told me how to make it. I wrote it down on the first thing I could lay my hands on—the back of a shopping list. That's where it is to this day. I just thumb through my recipe box until I see that really scruffy piece of folded notebook paper, and I know I've found it.

I must admit I took Linda's recipe and ran with it. I've served her spread for brunch on mini-bagels and as an appetizer on good crackers and I've given it away as a hostess gift every now and then. I've even sold it.

Whenever the spirit moves me (about every five years or so), I have a craft show at my house. In addition to all my handcrafted items, I sell "Gourmet Goodies" from my kitchen. Of course I make Linda's salmon spread for the occasion. It never fails to sell out first.

We moved to South Carolina in 1998, and I introduced my new southern friends to this New York specialty. The results were predictable. They couldn't get enough of it, either. This extraordinary spread will make your friends think you're a kitchen genius. At first taste they'll probably turn around, say, "Wow!", and ask for the recipe. Be nice like Linda. Give it to them.

Linda's Smoked Salmon Spread*

12 ounce container whipped cream cheese
1/4 pound smoked Nova Scotia lox, diced
3 or 4 scallions, chopped
2 tablespoons capers

Mix cream cheese with diced lox. Add scallions and capers and mash together with a strong fork until ingredients are blended together. Refrigerate until ready to use.

*Be sure to mix the ingredients by hand. A food processor will ruin the consistency of it and, according to Linda, will turn it into a green mess.

Makes 2 cups

Joy grew up to be a Jefferson High School cheerleader! (1961)
At the age of four she knew she belonged on the field with the players, the coaches, and the band.

Game Day Ham and Cheese Spread

If you love football like I do, January is probably one of your favorite months of the year. First are the college bowl games, followed by the NFC and AFC playoff games, and finally the Super Bowl in early February. It just doesn't get any better than that.

I attended my first football game when I was four years old. The principal of our local junior high school, Mr. Cook, and his daughter Sally took me. Mr. Cook was a member of our church and a family friend.

The game was a Friday night high school game at Victory Stadium in my hometown of Roanoke, Virginia. There was an air of excitement that even a four-year-old could sense. The Jefferson Senior High School "Magicians" were playing, bands were marching, people were cheering, the lights were bright, and the autumn air was crisp. Armed with cotton candy in one fist and a cowbell in the other, I had the time of my life. The Magicians won and I was hooked on football.

This early exposure to the game has had a lasting affect on me. At the age of four I decided I wanted to be a cheerleader. I knew I belonged down on the field with the players, the coaches, and the band. Well, guess what? In high school, I did become a cheerleader for the Jefferson Magicians, and it was every bit as exciting as I thought it would be.

My love of the game has never waivered. On Super Bowl Sunday, you'll find me in front of the television with the guys watching the game—not in another room playing cards, or watching a movie with the girls.

My interest in the sport has not gone unnoticed by my husband. Years ago, he gave me a Hallmark card that listed all of my best qualities, the most important being that I had "adequate sports knowledge". I consider this high praise indeed.

Even if you're not a football fan, go to a Super Bowl party for the food. It's predictably good. If you want to take a dish that's easy to make and sure to please, try one called "Game Day Ham and Cheese Spread". I stole this recipe from a friend who served it at a tailgate party. This football-shaped cheese ball with deviled ham as the secret ingredient is a guaranteed winner.

Game Day Ham and Cheese Spread

Two 8 ounce packages low fat cream cheese
10 ounce package extra sharp cheddar cheese
4 ½ ounce can deviled ham
1 small grated onion
Walnuts or pecans, finely chopped

Combine cream cheese and cheddar cheese with a mixer or in a food processor until well blended.

Add ham and onion. Mix well. Chill mixture. Form into the shape of a football. Roll in chopped nuts. Refrigerate.

Serve with crackers.

Mother's Wedding—October 15, 1930
They all had the olive cheese ball recipe-probably under their enormous bouquets

Mother's Olive Cheese Balls

As fashion trends go, I've learned that if you hold onto something long enough it'll come back into style. For example, bellbottom jeans of the 1970s resurfaced as flared jeans and pedal pushers from the 1950s returned as Capri pants. Cute little ballerina flats made a comeback, as did oversized sunglasses and peace symbols. And the beat goes on....

There are things I hope never to see again, of course. The dreaded beehive hairdo, for instance. Whose hideous idea was that anyway?

The same trends happen with food. What's old becomes new again in many cases. People sometimes crave foods they grew up with. I'm a perfect example.

I needed an appetizer to take to a cocktail party recently and thumbed through my recipe file. The minute I came to Mother's olive cheese ball recipe, I knew I had to make some. I was suddenly in the mood for this old favorite from my childhood.

Judging from the age of her recipe, my mother must have gotten it when she was a bride. All of her sisters had the recipe too. Whenever there was a family party, olive cheese balls were on the table.

When I arrived at the cocktail party, it turned out I wasn't the only person who craved an olive cheese ball. The plate was empty in a hurry. Apparently a warm cheese crust around a little green olive is irresistible to most folks.

I'm sure my mother would have been pleased. After all, the same thing happened when she made them in 1930. Apparently the old adage is true—what goes around, comes around. Welcome back, little olive cheese balls!

Mother's Olive Cheese Balls

2 sticks butter
5 cups grated extra sharp cheddar cheese
2 ½ cups flour
1 ½ teaspoon salt
2 ½ teaspoons paprika
1 small jar (5.75 ounces) pitted green olives, drained and patted dry

Cream the cheese and the butter by hand. Gradually add the remaining ingredients and mix well. Chill.

Flatten about a tablespoon of the cheese mixture between your palms and wrap it around each olive. Place olives on a cookie sheet and keep in the refrigerator until ready to put them in the oven.

Bake at 400 degrees for 15 minutes. Serve warm.

Note – After assembling the cheese balls and placing them on a cookie sheet, you can put them in the freezer instead of the refrigerator. Once frozen, store them in a freezer bag for future use. Just pop them from the freezer into a hot oven for a quick appetizer.

Yields about 60

Mother (Martha Davis)—1960
On her aged and spattered recipe card, it says "Serves 1,000". One Cheerio at a time.

Mother's Nuts and Bolts

My mother made a delicious snack that was listed as "Cereal Canapé" on her recipe card. It was an addictive mix of seasoned cereals and pretzels. She baked it slowly with a terrific mixture of butter, Worcestershire sauce and Tabasco stirred into it, and plenty of garlic salt, garlic powder, and parmesan cheese sprinkled over it.

This was long before something called Chex Mix ever hit the grocery shelves. Mother's mix had the same ingredients—Cheerios, Corn Chex, and pretzels—but she also put peanuts in hers. I think her old fashioned version of this now popular snack is much better than the current one. She called it "Nuts and Bolts"—the Cheerios were the bolts, and the nuts were, well, the nuts.

I love to make Nuts and Bolts, especially at Christmas. I still make tins of them for my children, even though they're all grown up. You simply don't outgrow your taste for something this good. I'm a perfect example.

When I make Nut and Bolts, I leave out the peanuts, so I guess you'd have to call my version, "Bolts and Stuff".

I have no idea how many this recipe serves. On Mother's aged and spattered recipe card, she's written "serves 1,000," which might be a little overstated. All I know is that no matter how much I make, it disappears. Once you taste Mother's Nuts and Bolts, you'll understand why.

Mother's Nuts and Bolts

2 sticks butter
6 tablespoons Worcestershire sauce
6 shakes Tabasco sauce (at least—I use more)
14 ounce box of Cheerios
14 ounce box of Corn Chex
16 ounce bag of pretzels (I use about 14 ounces)
Peanuts (optional)
Parmesan cheese (lots)
Garlic salt (plenty)
Garlic powder (a whole bunch)

Melt butter in a small saucepan. Add Worcestershire and Tabasco. Spread the Cheerios, Corn Chex, pretzels, and nuts (if you like) in 2 large flat pans. (I use the bottoms of broiler pans).

Spoon the butter mixture over it a little at a time, stirring well to coat the cereal. Sprinkle liberally with the cheese, garlic salt, and garlic powder.

Bake in a 300-degree oven for an hour, stirring every 15 minutes. Sprinkle with more cheese, salt, and garlic powder every time you stir it.

Remove from oven and let cool. Store in airtight containers to keep it fresh.

Judy and Kirby
Judy swore by dilly beans so I knew they had to be good. Plus, the dog liked them.

Dilly Beans

If you want to get a jump-start on Christmas presents, start in the summer. It's the perfect time to stock your pantry shelves with homemade gifts from the garden.

While fruits and vegetables are at their peak, take advantage of the opportunity. Make soups, stews, sauces, jellies, and anything else you can think of while the getting is good.

Dilled vegetables are among my summer specialties. I've dilled all kinds of vegetables, but my favorite is green beans. The beans hold up well in the canning process, look attractive in the jar, and are delicious as an appetizer or on an antipasto tray. These little treats are also reasonably addictive. It's almost impossible to eat just one.

My friend, Judy Morton, introduced me to dilly beans in the early 1980s. Judy is intuitive, well versed on a variety of topics, and has always been on the cutting edge of the latest trends. In other words, she just plain knows stuff. She swore by dilly beans so I knew they must be good.

Judy not only gave me a jar as a gift but also found the recipe for them in a really old cookbook that she had. She copied the page that featured the dilly bean recipe and sent it to me. I still use that well-worn, spattered page as my guide.

Making dilly beans is easy, but there are a few rules to follow. You have to start out with good fresh beans that are nice and crisp. The beans have to be straight, not curved. The curved ones won't fit in the jar, so this is an important detail.

It's time consuming to pick through a big pile of beans looking for only straight ones, but you have to do it. Pay no attention to the strange looks you get from fellow shoppers. They don't know what they're missing.

When you're finished making the beans, tie a pretty ribbon around each jar and add a fancy label. Relax. You're all set for any gift-giving opportunity that arises.

Even those "impossible to shop for" people will love them. After all, this is not just any gift. A homemade gift from your kitchen is also a gift from your heart. That's a winner every time.

Dilly Beans*

4 pounds fresh green beans
6 tablespoons salt
3 cups white vinegar
3 cups water
1/2 teaspoon dill seeds, per pint
1/2 mustard seeds, per pint
3 whole peppercorns, per pint
1 clove garlic, per pint
Sprigs of fresh dill for garnish

Put seasonings into clean, hot jars. Trim beans to ½ inch less than the height of the canning jar. Put beans into the jars, packing them tightly. Combine salt, vinegar, and water. Bring to a boil.

Using a funnel, carefully pour boiling liquid into jars, leaving ½ inch of headspace. Beans must be completely covered with water. Add sprig of fresh dill to each jar. Seal tightly with sterilized lids.

Place jars in a large pot of boiling water and process in the boiling water bath for 10 minutes. Remove and cool. The lids will make a popping sound and will be slightly indented when the seal is complete.

*You can use this same recipe to dill lots of other vegetables. I can recommend carrot sticks, asparagus, cauliflower, or green tomato slices (placed horizontally in the jar), but try whatever you like. Be creative.

Makes 7 pints

Joy and Peggy
"Quick! Look cute! A guy is coming this way. Maybe he can get us down from here!"

Peggy's Hot Pepper Jelly

There's a reason why summer is the time to make jams and jellies. It's a no–brainer. That's when most of the fruits and berries are at their peak.

As my grandmother used to say, you "strike while the iron is hot". My father's version of that, "make hay while the sun shines" is appropriate here too. Now go pull out those canning jars, and let's get started!

Hot pepper jelly is my favorite. My recipe for this spicy concoction came from my good friend, Peggy Swink. It's on a bright green card in my recipe box, so it's easy to find. I reach for that green card every summer and think of her while I'm sweating over a hot stove making pepper jelly.

Making pepper jelly is a good thing because the end result is so delicious, but sometimes the preparation gets a little dicey. NEVER EVER make the mistake of touching the hot peppers, and then rubbing your eyes, or any other sensitive part of your body. Trust me, it's excruciatingly painful. You won't make the mistake more than once, if you're lucky.

This southern specialty just can't be beat when served on a cracker with cream cheese. Every good southern girl knows that this peppery spread is a must for any decent appetizer tray south of the Mason-Dixon line.

Enjoy this delicacy, but watch out—after tasting it, you might have a sudden urge to jump up and sing a few bars of "Dixie".

Peggy's Hot Pepper Jelly

¼ cup chopped Cayenne peppers
1 ½ cup chopped green bell peppers
6 ½ cups sugar
1 ½ cups vinegar
6 ounce bottle Certo (liquid fruit pectin)
Green food coloring

Put peppers in the blender with a little water, and blend until liquefied. Mix sugar, vinegar, and the blended peppers together in a very large saucepan. Bring to a rolling boil and boil for 3 minutes. Add Certo and boil for 1 minute.

Remove from heat. Skim off the foam with a metal spoon for 5 minutes. Stir in a few drops of green food coloring.

Pour into hot dry sterilized jars and seal.

Makes approximately 7 pints

INDEX

PASTA

VEGETABLES, CASSEROLES, AND SIDE DISHES

SALADS AND SALAD DRESSINGS

SOUPS

BREADS

BRUNCH, CHEESE AND SPREADS

APPETIZERS

About the Author

Joy Smith lives in Fort Mill, South Carolina, with her husband and a quirky cat. She loves cooking, entertaining, traveling, playing tennis and bridge, riding horses, gardening when it's not too hot (which is almost never in South Carolina), and enjoying good wine. Her sense of adventure has taken her to Antarctica on a National Geographic Expedition, skydiving, climbing mountains, and searching for the perfect roller coaster.

Joy participated as a sous chef on the Food Network show "Ready...Set...Cook!"; was a guest chef on the NBC show Charlotte Today; taught a class, "From the Garden to the Table"; and wrote a popular cooking column, "Cooking With Joy," for ten years. Readers have enjoyed her stories and recipes, which have been featured in several magazines and newspapers. You will be entertained by them as you read, "Tell Me a Story, I'll Bake You a Cake."

Edwards Brothers Malloy
Ann Arbor MI. USA
May 3, 2017